I DESERVE A DONUT

And Other Lies That Make You Eat

BARB RAVELING

D0973483

Cover Illustration: Volha Sakovich (v0lha at istock.com)
Initial Cover Design: KCgraphicdesign @fiverr.com
Back and Final Cover Design: Teddi Black
Author Photo: Abby Raveling

This book is not intended as a substitute for the advice of
professional counselors. If you are struggling with a serious
issue, please do so under the guidance of a professional
counselor and/or physician.

All scripture quotations, unless otherwise indicated, are taken
from the New American Standard Bible ®, Copyright © 1960,
1962, 1963, 1968, 1971, 1972, 1973, 1975, 1977, 1995 by the
Lockman Foundation. Used by permission.
www.Lockman.org

Scripture quotations marked NIV are taken from the Holy
Bible, New International Version®, NIV®. Copyright © 1973,
1978, 1984, 2011 by Biblica, Inc.™ Used by permission of
Zondervan. All rights reserved
worldwide. www.zondervan.com The "NIV" and "New
International Version" are trademarks registered in the United
States Patent and Trademark Office by Biblica, Inc.™

ISBN: 0-9802243-0-6
ISBN-13: 978-0-9802243-0-6

To Scott, Jenny, Abby, and Tanya.

Thank you for continuing to give me advice through countless rounds of "Which question do you think is better? This one or that one?" I appreciate you guys!

Contents

Lies that Make You Eat

Emotions That Make You Eat

Preface

I began writing *I Deserve a Donut (And Other Lies That Make You Eat)* several years ago. At the time I didn't know I was writing a book. I was just writing questions and collecting Bible verses.

I wouldn't have taken it any further if I hadn't been teaching a group of teenagers at the time. One of the boys in the class said, "You should put these questions on an app. Call it iBarb!"

I laughed. That would be fun—but of course I would never be capable of making an iPhone app.

Still, I thought, it was an interesting idea: an app that wouldn't just *track* behavior, but that would help you renew your mind so you wouldn't even want to *do* your behavior.

The idea would have stayed in the back of my mind except for one coincidence: I have a son who programs iPhone apps for a living. So I called him and nervously started working on the project.

Half a year later (after writing and rewriting the questions what seemed like a million times), *I Deserve a Donut* was ready to go. I put the app on the market and then I realized, not everyone has an iPhone. I don't have an iPhone! I had to buy an iPod just to test the app.

At the time, I wasn't capable of putting it out in any other form because I was such a procrastinator, and it seemed like too much work.

But then God began to change me. I used the questions in this book to go to Him for help with procrastination, and slowly but surely, He began to work on me from the inside out.

What you have in your hands is a result of the power of God. He took this I-want-life-to-be-easy procrastinator and is transforming me through the renewing of the mind.

When we begin any endeavor—whether it's working on an eating problem, a procrastination problem, or any other problem—we start out believing the lie that *we will never get over this.*

I felt that way about food seven years ago, and I felt that way about procrastination and getting things done up to about nine months ago. But thanks be to God, He is capable of changing us.

Transformation is messy. It feels like too much work, too much time—and too much failure. We're bombarded by "I'll never change, anyway, so why bother?" sorts of thoughts. We want to give up.

That's why we so desperately need to go to God for help—because we can't do it by ourselves.

I Deserve a Donut is a tool you can use to go to God for help with eating. It contains questions and Bible verses you can use to have a conversation with Him about life and food.

The questions and Bible verses will help you change your desires in the moment of temptation so you won't even *want* to break your boundaries.

If you're already familiar with the renewing of the mind and boundaries in eating, you can dive right into this book.

If you're not familiar with them, check out the appendix at the back of the book, the free weight loss Bible studies at barbraveling.com, or my Bible study, *Freedom from Emotional Eating.*

My prayer is that God will bless you through the questions and Bible verses in this book.

How to Use This Book

Have you ever met a person who doesn't really care about food? Who actually *forgets* to eat?

My husband is one of those people. He can walk by a fresh cinnamon roll, straight from the oven, oozing with goodness, and say, "Hmm, that looks good."

He keeps walking because it wouldn't cross his mind to eat when he wasn't hungry.

I, on the other hand, walk by that same cinnamon roll, and think, *That looks like the most incredible cinnamon roll in the whole wide world. I should eat it right now this very minute.*

And then I do.

So here's my question. Is there hope for those of us who want to eat everything in sight?

Or do we have to go through life trying to muster up every bit of self-control we can get our hands on, just to hold on to some semblance of normalcy in the weight department?

There is hope.

It's found in a Bible verse: "And do not be conformed to this world, but be transformed by the renewing of your mind" (Romans 12:a).

In this verse Paul tells us that change begins on the inside, through the renewing of the mind. So the best way to approach weight loss isn't to focus on saying no to the cinnamon roll.

It's to focus on **changing the thoughts** that make us want to say yes.

I Deserve a Donut is a book that will help you change the way you think about food so you can lose weight *and* keep it off.

Here's how it works: If you look at the table of contents,

11

you'll see two sections: *Lies That Make You Eat* and *Emotions That Make You Eat.* Take a minute to look at that first category. It lists twenty different lies that make us eat too much.

Do you see how the lie in Good Food Eating—*That looks good. I should eat it*—matches up with what I was thinking when I walked by the cinnamon roll?

If you go to Good Food Eating, you'll see nine questions. The questions are designed to point out the lies you believe about food that make you want to eat when you're not hungry.

Use the questions to have a little conversation with God about your temptation. You could even pretend that He's asking you the questions.

Let's give this a try right now with the situation we talked about earlier. We'll go through the questions and see how they would change our thoughts about that cinnamon roll.

Good Food Questions

1. On a scale of 1 to 10, how great do you think this food would taste?

Usually when we see a food from our favorite food category, we automatically think, *That's so great, I have to have it.* But the truth is, not all treats are created equally.

Some are a 10 on a scale of 1 to 10, but some are only a 6 or 7. The first question in Good Food Eating should make you stop and think, *Is this really going to be as good as I think?* If it isn't, don't eat it.

You might even want to consider making a rule: If it's not good for me, I won't eat it unless it's at least a 9 on a scale of 1 to 10.

2. How much would you need to eat to be satisfied?

Hopefully, the answer to this question is "One cinnamon roll." If the answer is, "I can eat and eat and eat and *never* be satisfied," then you're probably eating for emotional reasons. At that point, you would turn to the emotional eating questions and work through those instead.

3. Can you eat this food without breaking your boundaries?

When we see really great food, our mind is often so consumed by the food that we can't think straight. We just think, *I have to have that food!*

This question breaks us out of our reverie. *Wait a minute. Can I eat this without breaking my boundaries?* If the answer is no, we're asked to think back to why we have boundaries.

It's always good to remember why we have boundaries. If we take the time to remember what life is like both with and without boundaries, we'll actually *want* to follow them. (Note: If you're not familiar with the word *boundaries*, see the appendix.)

4. How often will you follow your boundaries if you only follow them on the days you feel like following them? (Be honest.)

For some odd reason, we think it will be easier to follow our boundaries tomorrow. This question brings us back to reality. It's *never* easy to follow boundaries. So we might as well follow them today.

5. Do you think God wants you to follow your boundaries? Why or why not?

When you go through the questions, be sure to fully answer the whys and why nots.

In order for us to change the way we think, we need to actually think! That means putting some effort into our thought life. The whys and why nots will help you put some effort into your thought life.

Does God really care if you follow your boundaries? Why or why not? Try to answer that question as fully as possible. Here's how I would answer it:

Yes, God wants me to follow my boundaries because He knows I can become obsessed with food. He also knows that I turn to food for emotional support. And He knows that I procrastinate with food.

God wants me to love *Him*—not food—with all my heart. He wants me to turn to Him—not food—for emotional support. And He wants me to turn to Him—not food—for help with writing.

Boundaries help me turn to Him rather than food, so yes, I think God wants me to have boundaries with food. Do you see how this question would help me start thinking, *Hmm, maybe I shouldn't have that cinnamon roll, after all?*

6. Are boundaries easy to follow or do you usually have to give up something to follow them?

Usually, I walk through life thinking everything should be easy. This question pulls me up short. It's not easy to follow boundaries. Of course. I keep forgetting. I need this question to remind me that I shouldn't expect this to be easy.

7. What will you have to give up to follow your boundaries this time?

In this case, I need to give up the cinnamon roll.

8. What will your life and body look like a couple of months down the road if you develop the habit of consistently following your boundaries?

This is another one of those questions you'll need to answer as fully as possible. Here's what will happen if you consistently follow your boundaries for two or three months: You'll lose weight. You'll feel better. You'll have more energy.

You'll wake up in the morning without regret. And you'll have hope that you can actually break free from the control of food. Just listing all those benefits makes me want to follow my own boundaries.

9. When you think of all you'll gain, is it worth the sacrifice?

By the time I get to this question, if I've taken the time to fully think through the answers to the previous questions, I'll actually *want* to say no to the cinnamon roll. The questions are a way to renew my mind—to see life and food from a biblical perspective.

Going to God for Help

The questions are also a way to grow closer to God. When you look at the example above, it might not look like I'm talking to God. That's because you don't see what goes on *off* the paper.

When I renew my mind, I often set my pen down to visit with God. To thank Him. To mull over His Word. To ask Him a question. And to soak in His love.

The renewing of the mind is like a counseling session. A time to visit with our Father about life. It's an incredible time of fellowship, but it's also a time of conviction. It often brings me to my knees in repentance as I become aware of my sin.

As you renew your mind, remember that God is a loving Father who wants to help you, not a perfectionist parent who wants to condemn you (Romans 8:1).

Remember also that Jesus has been in your shoes. He's struggled with every temptation you have (Hebrews 4:15), so He is perfectly suited to help you work through your problems. And finally, remember that the Holy Spirit is your teacher (John 14:26), and He wants to help.

How to Know Which Questions to Use

In the beginning, it might be hard to know which questions to use. This will get easier with practice. Usually, you can use more than one set.

For example, if you feel like you *deserve* the cinnamon roll, use the entitlement questions. If you're avoiding a job, use the procrastination questions. And if you just want a little excitement in your life, use the boredom questions.

You'll also notice that there is a whole section on emotional eating. If you're eating for emotional reasons, try to deal with the situation itself rather than just your desire to eat.

For example, let's say you're annoyed with a family member, and it's making you want to eat. Use the anger questions to renew your mind. If you get rid of the emotion that's driving you to eat, you'll also get rid of the desire to eat. If you don't have time to work through the issue, use the emotional eating questions.

When To Use the Questions

There are three different ways you can approach the questions. You can use them a) whenever you're tempted to break your boundaries, b) whenever you actually break your boundaries, or c) once or twice a day.

1. Before you break your boundaries.

If you can make yourself do it, this is the best approach. Go through a set of questions whenever you're tempted to break your boundaries. Answer the questions in your journal, if possible. If not, just do it in your head.

The purpose of the questions is to renew your mind with truth so you won't even *want* to break your boundaries. If you notice your desires changing halfway through the questions, there's no need to answer all of them.

2. After you break your boundaries.

It may seem counterproductive, but go ahead and do the questions even if you've already broken your boundaries.

This will serve two purposes: First, it will make you want to follow your boundaries for the next hour or two. And second, it will help you change the way you think about food.

Every little bit of truth you put into your system helps— even if you put it in after you break your boundaries.

If you use this method, try to remember what you were thinking before you broke your boundaries. Then choose a set of questions to deal with those thoughts. If you can't remember what you were thinking, use the failure questions.

3. Once or twice a day.

A friend of mine lost over one hundred pounds using these questions, and rather than using them every time she felt like breaking her boundaries, she just started at the beginning and went through them, one set at a time.

She answered the questions in her journal and thought about them throughout the day. God used the questions to change the way she thought about food, which helped her stick to her boundaries and lose weight.

How To Use the Bible Verses

Do you remember how Jesus used Bible verses when Satan tempted Him in the desert (Matthew 4:1-11)? We can use Bible verses the same way.

Whenever you're tempted to eat, throw a Bible verse at the thought or the lie that's making you want to eat.

Here's an example. Let's say I'm back in the kitchen, looking at that cinnamon roll. If I stop looking at the cinnamon roll and start looking at Romans 13:14, I'll be more likely to say no to temptation.

Romans 13:14 *But put on the Lord Jesus Christ, and make no provision for the flesh in regard to its lusts.*

Romans 13:14 would remind me, "I'm lusting after that cinnamon roll, and God doesn't want me to lust. I need to be careful not to make a provision for my flesh. I better follow my boundaries."

1 Corinthians 6:12 *All things are lawful for me, but not all things are profitable. All things are lawful for me, but I will not be mastered by anything.*

Or I could look at 1 Corinthians 6:12 and say, "Hmm, all things are lawful, so I *could* eat this cinnamon roll, but it wouldn't be profitable. If I eat this, I'll be going down that rocky road of breaking my boundaries, and that never ends well. You know what? I'm not going to be mastered by this cinnamon roll. I'm going to follow my boundaries."

Do you see how these Bible verses renew your mind and change your desires? The incredible thing about the Bible is that it works. It applies to all of life. It is life changing.

Are You Ready to Begin?

One of the things I love about the questions and Bible verses is that they provide a path for me to go to God for help with my problems. My prayer is that they will do the same for you.

If you'd like a Bible study that goes along with the questions, look for *Taste for Truth: A 30 Day Bible Study*, which I hope to publish by January 2014.

The best way to learn how to use this book is to just jump in and give it a try. Why don't you get started right now with your first set of questions and Bible verses?

Appearance Eating

If you're eating because:

1. **You feel like you *have* to be skinny:** see greed/lust questions and Bible verses.

2. **You feel like you'll never be skinny:** see hopeless or tired of the struggle eating.

3. **You had a bad weigh-in:** see bad scale eating.

4. **You look fat :** see discontentment, feeling inadequate, or self-condemnation.

5. **You're afraid to meet people because of how you look:** see insecurity/social situations, self-condemnation, or worry.

6. **You're worried someone will reject or condemn you because of your weight:** see worry, people pleasing, living up to expectations, or feeling rejected and condemned.

7. **You're worried that you're not going to look good for a special occasion:** see worry, discontentment, feeling inadequate, or self-condemnation.

Bible Verses

Psalm 139:13-15 For You formed my inward parts; You wove me in my mother's womb. I will give thanks to You, for I am fearfully and wonderfully made; Wonderful are Your works, And my soul knows it very well. My frame was not hidden from You when I was made in secret, and skillfully wrought in the depths of the earth.

1 Samuel 16:7b For God sees not as man sees, for man looks at the outward appearance, but the Lord looks at the heart.

John 6:27 Do not work for the food which perishes, but for the food which endures to eternal life, which the Son of Man will give to you, for on Him the Father, God, has set His seal.

Philippians 4:11 Not that I speak from want, for I have learned to be content in whatever circumstances I am.

Ephesians 2:10 For we are His workmanship, created in Christ Jesus for good works, which God prepared beforehand so that we would walk in them.

Romans 8:1 Therefore there is now no condemnation for those who are in Christ Jesus.

1 Thessalonians 5:18 In everything give thanks; for this is God's will for you in Christ Jesus.

1 Peter 2:9 But you are a chosen race, a royal priesthood, a holy nation, a people for God's own possession, so that you may proclaim the excellencies of Him who has called you out of darkness into His marvelous light.

1 Peter 3:3-4 Your adornment must not be merely external— braiding the hair, and wearing gold jewelry, or putting on dresses; but let it be the hidden person of the heart, with the imperishable quality of a gentle and quiet spirit, which is precious in the sight of God.

Tips

Because we live in a culture that is obsessed with appearance and defines beautiful as "skinny," it's easy to think we have to be skinny to be acceptable.

This isn't true. God cares more about our insides than our outsides, and He loves us in our "as is" state. If you're tempted to see yourself through the culture's eyes, here's an activity that will help:

Stand in front of the mirror once a day and say (or shout), "Hollywood has no right to tell me I'm unacceptable when the Living God, King of the Universe, says that I AM acceptable!!"

It sounds a little embarrassing, but it works (although you may want to do it when no one else is home).

It also helps to focus on the spiritual goal of breaking free from the control of food rather than the physical goal of losing weight. See the tips in Failure Eating for more about this.

Bad Scale Eating

1. What were you expecting to lose this week?
2. Do you think that was a realistic expectation? Why or why not?
3. Based on your past experiences with weight loss, does your weight usually go down in a nice, neat, always-predictable curve? If not, what usually happens?
4. Is it more important to lose weight, or to consistently renew your mind so you change the way you think about food? Explain.
5. On a scale of 1 to 10, how diligent have you been about renewing your mind this week?
6. What would you gain by giving up your hopes for a quick fix to this problem and accepting the fact that this isn't going to be easy?
7. What do you think God wants to teach you through this trial?
8. Is there anything you need to accept?
9. What can you thank God for in this situation?

Bible Verses

Galatians 6:9 Let us not lose heart in doing good, for in due time we will reap if we do not grow weary.

Philippians 1:6 For I am confident of this very thing, that He who began a good work in you will perfect it until the day of Christ Jesus.

Philippians 4:11 Not that I speak from want, for I have learned to be content in whatever circumstances I am.

Romans 8:28 And we know that God causes all things to work together for good to those who love God, to those who are called according to His purpose.

1 Thessalonians 5:18 In everything give thanks; for this is God's will for you in Christ Jesus.

See also: discontentment, appearance eating, denial eating, and failure eating.

Tips

The easiest way to get rid of bad scale eating is to get rid of the scale. You could get rid of the scale for good, for a few months, or just have someone hide it from you for a week at a time so you're not tempted to weigh yourself during the week.

If you decide to keep the scale, try to think of your weight as a weight range rather than a number. For example, instead of saying that you weigh 150 pounds, say that your weight range is 150-152.

This is a more realistic way of looking at weight since it often fluctuates even when you're following your boundaries. It's also a more helpful way to look at your weight as you won't be tempted to eat in despair when you step on the scale and find that you're 152.

If you consistently fail to lose weight even though you've been following your boundaries, check out denial eating just to make sure you're not eating more than you think you are. If you're still not losing what you think you should be losing, consult a weight loss expert.

Boredom Eating

1. What do you feel like eating?
2. Will you break a boundary if you eat that?
   a. **Yes:** If so, which boundary will you break? Is that a good boundary? Explain.
   b. **No:** If not, will you be more likely to break your boundaries later if you eat this? Why or why not?
3. How much time do you need to fill until your next meal or snack?
4. Would eating be a good way to fill this time?
5. What are some other things you could do with this block of time? List a few ideas.
6. What would be the best use of your time right now?
7. What would you gain by using your time this way?
8. Is there anything you need to accept?

Note: Can you think of any ways you could use this time to show love to God or the people in your life?

Bible Verses

Psalm 18:29 For by You I can run upon a troop; and by my God I can leap over a wall.

2 Corinthians 12:9a And He has said to me, "My grace is sufficient for you, for power is perfected in weakness."

Philippians 1:21 For to me, to live is Christ and to die is gain.

Philippians 4:19 And my God will supply all your needs according to His riches in glory in Christ Jesus.

1 Thessalonians 5:18 In everything give thanks; for this is God's will for you in Christ Jesus.

1 Timothy 6:7-8 For we brought nothing into the world, and we can take nothing out of it. But if we have food and clothing, we will be content with that.

1 John 3:16 We know love by this, that He laid down His life for us; and we ought to lay down our lives for the brethren.

Tips

The easiest way to eliminate boredom eating is to get an exciting life. Unfortunately, this isn't always possible nor is it always what God wants! There are all kinds of exciting things we could do that God wouldn't be happy about.

If you struggle with boredom eating, spend some time talking to God about it. How do you think He wants you to spend your time? If you have lots of time on your hands, what could you do to reach out to others with your time? What could you do to serve?

If you're already doing what He wants you to do, work on changing your attitude. This is what I wish I would have done back in the days when I was homeschooling my four kids and they were all little.

That could have been a wonderful opportunity for growth if I had used that time to see life from God's perspective. Unfortunately, I spend many of those winters being discontent because my life wasn't as exciting as I wanted it to be.

Boredom is a trial that can either bring you closer to God or further from Him. Use it to bring you closer.

Careless Eating

1. What do you feel like eating?
2. Will you break a boundary if you eat that?
   a. If so, which boundary will break?
   b. Is that a good boundary? Why or why not?
3. In the past, have you been able to eat a bite here or there and still maintain discipline in your eating?
4. What usually happens when you get sloppy with your boundaries?
5. Is your life better or worse with boundaries? Why?
6. Are boundaries easy to follow, or do you usually have to give up something to follow them?
7. What will you have to give up to follow your boundary this time?
8. When you think of all you'll gain by living a life free from the control of food, is it worth the sacrifice?

Bible Verses

Mark 14:38 Keep watching and praying that you may not come into temptation; the spirit is willing, but the flesh is weak.

Romans 13:14 But put on the Lord Jesus Christ, and make no provision for the flesh in regard to its lusts.

1 Corinthians 6:12 All things are lawful for me, but not all things are profitable. All things are lawful for me, but I will not be mastered by anything.

1 Timothy 4:7b Discipline yourself for the purpose of godliness.

1 Thessalonians 5:6 So then let us not sleep as others do, but let us be alert and sober.

1 Peter 5:8 Be of sober spirit, be on the alert. Your adversary, the devil, prowls around like a roaring lion, seeking someone to devour.

Tips

Careless eating is different than just forgetting about your boundaries. With careless eating, the mindset is that the boundaries are mere guidelines. Yes, you try to stick to them, but it's not a big deal if you break them either.

The truth is that the sloppier your boundaries are, the more likely you'll be to give them up altogether.

If you're having trouble *remembering* your boundaries, try putting sticky notes in your kitchen until you remember them.

Denial Eating

1. What do you feel like eating?
2. Will you break a boundary if you eat this?
   a. **Yes:** Which boundary will you break? How were you planning to justify it? Is your justification valid? Why or why not?
   b. **No:** Will you be more likely to break your boundaries later if you eat this now? If so, what are the chances you'll be able to eat this without regretting it later?
3. Are boundaries easy to follow, or do you usually have to give up something to follow them?
4. What will you have to give up to follow your boundaries this time?
5. What will you gain if you follow your boundaries?
6. When you think of what you'll gain, is it worth the sacrifice?

Bible Verses

Psalm 120:2 Deliver my soul, O Lord, from lying lips, from a deceitful tongue.

Romans 13:14 But put on the Lord Jesus Christ, and make no provision for the flesh in regard to its lusts.

1 Thessalonians 5:6 So then let us not sleep as others do, but let us be alert and sober.

1 Thessalonians 5:21 But examine everything carefully; hold fast to that which is good.

1 Peter 5:8 Be of sober spirit, be on the alert. Your adversary, the devil, prowls around like a roaring lion, seeking someone to devour.

Tips

There are two ways we engage in denial eating. First, we tell ourselves we're following our boundaries when we're really not. And second, we tell ourselves we're not eating that much when we really are. Here are a few examples of denial eating:

1. We say we're hungry when we're really not.
2. We count the calories we *eat*, but ignore the calories we drink.
3. We say it's part of our meal when it was really just an afterthought.
4. We count the food we eat when we sit down for a meal but ignore the food we eat when we're standing in front of the stove.
5. We count the *cookies* we eat but ignore the dough we eat when we're making the cookies.

If we want to lose weight and keep it off, we'll need to be honest about what we're eating. If you've been faithfully and honestly following your boundaries for several weeks and still aren't losing weight, consult a weight loss expert.

Emotional Eating

1. What's going on in your life right now that's making you want to eat?
2. What emotion are you experiencing?
3. Will eating make you feel better? If so, for how long?
4. Will eating solve your problems?
5. Will eating create any new problems? Explain.
6. What do your boundaries protect you from?
7. Do you need protection today?
8. What do you think God wants to teach you through this trial?
9. Is there anything you need to accept?
10. What can you thank God for in this situation?

Bible Verses

Psalm 3:3 But You, O Lord, are a shield about me, my glory, and the One who lifts my head.

Psalm 61:1-2 Hear my cry, O God; give heed to my prayer. From the end of the earth I call to You when my heart is faint; lead me to the rock that is higher than I.

Jeremiah 29:11-13 "For I know the plans I have for you," declares the Lord, "plans for welfare and not for calamity to give you a future and a hope. Then you will call upon Me and come and pray to Me, and I will listen to you. You will seek Me and find Me when you search for Me with all your heart."

Jeremiah 32:27 Behold, I am the Lord, the God of all flesh; is anything too difficult for Me?

Romans 5:3-4 And not only this, but we also exult in our tribulations, knowing that tribulation brings about perseverance; and perseverance, proven character; and proven character, hope.

Philippians 4:19 And my God will supply all your needs according to His riches in glory in Christ Jesus.

Philippians 4:11-13 Not that I speak from want, for I have learned to be content in whatever circumstances I am. I know how to get along with humble means, and I also know how to live in prosperity; in any and every circumstance I have learned the secret of being filled and going hungry, both of having abundance and suffering need. I can do all things through Him who strengthens me.

Hebrews 12:11 All discipline for the moment seems not to be joyful, but sorrowful; yet to those who have been trained by it, afterwards it yields the peaceful fruit of righteousness.

Tips

The telltale sign of emotional eating is that you feel driven to eat. You don't just see a brownie on the counter and want it; you go looking for the brownie because you need it.

Emotional eating is usually triggered by something else going on in your life, usually something bad. Sometimes the need to eat is all-consuming, and sometimes it's just a nagging little thought at the back of your mind.

The best way to break free from emotional eating is to get rid of the emotions that are driving you to eat. Ask yourself, "What emotion am I experiencing?" Then go through the questions and Bible verses for that emotion.

What usually happens when you take the time to work through the emotion is that your desire to eat will disappear. If you *don't* take the time, that emotion has to go somewhere. Usually, it goes to the kitchen looking for something to eat.

Entitlement Eating

1. What do you feel like eating?
2. Why do you feel like you have a right to eat in this particular situation?
3. Do you think God agrees with your outlook on life? Why or why not?
4. What usually happens when you live by your rights and your feelings in this area of your life?
5. Would your life be better if you gave up your rights and held life and food with open hands? Why or why not?
6. Are boundaries easy to follow or do you usually have to give up something to follow them?
7. What will you have to give up to follow your boundaries this time?
8. What will your life and body look like a few months down the road if you develop the habit of consistently following your boundaries?
9. When you think of all you'll gain, is it worth the sacrifice?

Bible Verses

Jeremiah 2:13 For My people have committed two evils: they have forsaken Me, the fountain of living waters, to hew for themselves cisterns, broken cisterns that can hold no water.

Romans 13:14 But put on the Lord Jesus Christ, and make no provision for the flesh in regard to its lusts.

Philippians 3:7 But whatever things were gain to me, those things I have counted as loss for the sake of Christ.

Philippians 3:18-19 For many walk, of whom I often told you, and now tell you even weeping, that they are enemies of the cross of Christ, whose end is destruction, whose god is their appetite, and whose glory is in their shame, who set their minds on earthly things.

Philippians 4:11 Not that I speak from want, for I have learned to be content in whatever circumstances I am.

Hebrews 12:4,7 You have not yet resisted to the point of shedding blood in your striving against sin; it is for discipline that you endure; God deals with you as with sons; for what son is there whom his father does not discipline?

James 4:6b God is opposed to the proud, but gives grace to the humble.

1 Peter 1:14-16 As obedient children, do not be conformed to the former lusts which were yours in your ignorance, but like the Holy One who called you, be holy yourselves also in all your behavior, because it is written, "You shall be holy, for I am holy."

Tips

It's hard to break free from entitlement eating because we hear the message everywhere we go: *Life should be fair. If she gets something, you should get something. You shouldn't have to suffer. You deserve the good life.*

The best way to break free from entitlement eating is to adopt a biblical perspective of life. God never said, "You deserve the good life, and of course you have a right to eat." Instead, He said, "If you want to follow me, you have to be willing to give up everything."

When we hold food with tightly clenched fists and say it's our *right* to eat, we're basically saying, "I deserve this, God, and

I'm not willing to give it up.

God says, "That food will never make you happy. Come to Me, and I'll give you the abundant life."

The more we hold food with open hands, willing to give up all things for God, the more content we'll be. If you want to gain victory over entitlement eating, learn to hold food with open hands.

Note: I'm not saying we should starve ourselves - just be willing to follow our boundaries!

Scripture references: Matthew 10:37-39, Luke 18:18-27, John 10:10.

Failure Eating

1. Are you one of those rare people who can follow your boundaries effortlessly and perfectly without ever breaking them?
   a. If not, what's the sad truth you'll have to accept right from the beginning?
2. Since you can't go back and change what you ate today, what do you think God wants you to do now?
   a. Forget about the boundaries the rest of the day and start fresh in the morning.
   b. Beat yourself up.
   c. Remember that you're in a spiritual battle. Continue to fight the battle with spiritual weapons, knowing that you'll fail at times. Be extra diligent with your weapons in the next 24 hours so you don't break your boundaries again.
3. Which option are you inclined to take? Why?
4. What are the odds you could take that option without regretting it later?
5. If you want to live a life with boundaries, will you have to stop breaking them at some point?
6. What would be the advantage of stopping today?
7. What will your life and body look like a few months down the road if you develop the habit of consistently following your boundaries?
8. When you think of what you'll gain, is it worth the sacrifice to follow your boundaries the rest of the day?

Bible verses

Romans 6:1-2 What shall we say then? Are we to continue in sin so that grace may increase? May it never be! How shall we who died to sin still live in it?

Romans 13:14 But put on the Lord Jesus Christ, and make no provision for the flesh in regard to its lusts.

Galatians 6:9 Let us not lose heart in doing good, for in due time we will reap if we do not grow weary.

Philippians 1:6 For I am confident of this very thing, that He who began a good work in you will perfect it until the day of Christ Jesus.

Hebrews 12:11 All discipline for the moment seems not to be joyful, but sorrowful; yet to those who have been trained by it, afterwards it yields the peaceful fruit of righteousness.

James 1:12 Blessed is the man who perseveres under trial; for once he has been approved, he will receive the crown of life, which the Lord has promised to those who love Him.

See also: hopeless eating, regret, tired of the struggle, and self-condemnation.

Tips

The best way to avoid failure eating is to renew your mind *every* time you break your boundaries—before you eat another bite. If you're beating yourself up, try the self-condemnation questions or the regret questions and Bible verses.

It also helps to focus on the spiritual battle (breaking free from the control of food) rather than the physical battle (losing weight).

Here's why: If you look at failure from a biblical perspective, it won't matter how much you just ate. Whether it was a hundred calories or three thousand, calories, your job is still the same: renew your mind so you can break free from the control of food.

If you look at failure from a physical perspective, however, it *will* matter how much you ate. Because you might have just blown your chances for being skinny—and *that* will make you want to eat in despair.

Another advantage of looking at failure from a biblical perspective is that God is a much more gracious and loving taskmaster than the world.

The world (at least the one in our minds) says *What?! You ate how much?? That's terrible, you loser!!! You're going to be fat for the rest of your life!!!*

God, on the other hand, says, *I understand how hard it is. I used to live there, remember? Don't despair. Just fill your mind with truth so you'll be less likely to do it next time. I don't condemn you, but I don't want you to keep eating either. Oh—and by the way—have I told you how much I love you lately?*

Try to renew your mind every time you break your boundaries before you eat another bite. This will help you avoid a binge.

Garbage Disposal Eating

1. On a scale of 1 to 10, how much do you like this food?
2. On a scale of 1 to 10, how much does your body need this food?
3. Are you able to give this food away or save it for later without being tempted by it? If so, that would be the best option. If not, answer the following questions.
4. Is feeding this food to a body that doesn't need it more noble than throwing it in the garbage can? Explain.
5. Is it still going to waste if you feed it to a body that doesn't need it? If so, would it be better to throw it away in your body or in the garbage can?
6. Is there anything you need to accept?

Tips

Garbage disposal eating usually happens one of two places: at home when you're clearing the table or at a restaurant when you have too much food on your plate.

If you struggle with this at home, try renewing your mind before you do the dishes.

If you tend to overeat at restaurants, try ordering a to-go container as soon as you order your food. When your food arrives, decide on a healthy amount to eat and put the rest in the box. This will help you avoid eating just because it's there to eat.

Good Food Eating

1. On a scale of 1 to 10, how great do you think this food would taste?
2. How much would you need to eat to be satisfied? *
3. Can you eat this food without breaking your boundaries?
    a. **No:** If not, which boundary will you break? Is that a good boundary? Why?
    b. **Yes:** If so, will you be more likely to break your boundaries later if you eat this now? Why or why not?
4. How often will you follow your boundaries if you only follow them on the days you feel like following them? (Be honest.)
5. Do you think God wants you to follow your boundaries? Why or why not?
6. Are boundaries easy to follow or do you usually have to give up something to follow them?
7. What will you have to give up to follow your boundaries this time?
8. What will your life and body look like a couple of months down the road if you develop the habit of consistently following your boundaries?
9. When you think of all you'll gain, is it worth the sacrifice?

* If your answer is "No amount will satisfy me," turn to the emotional eating questions.

Bible Verses

Luke 12:15 Then (Jesus) said to them, "Beware, and be on your guard against every form of greed; for not even when one has an abundance does his life consist of possessions."

Romans 13:14 But put on the Lord Jesus Christ, and make no provision for the flesh in regard to its lusts.

Philippians 4:11-12 Not that I speak from want, for I have learned to be content in whatever circumstances I am. I know how to get along with humble means, and I also know how to live in prosperity; in any and every circumstance I have learned the secret of being filled and going hungry, both of having abundance and suffering need.

Philippians 4:13 I can do all things through Him who strengthens me.

Hebrews 12:11 All discipline for the moment seems not to be joyful, but sorrowful; yet to those who have been trained by it, afterwards it yields the peaceful fruit of righteousness.

Tips

The key to overcoming good food eating is to realize that more is not necessarily better. At a certain point, the taste of food deteriorates.

Just think of eating a large cinnamon roll from your local bakery. The first bite is almost always a 10 on a scale of a 1 to 10, but at some point the taste will dwindle. Depending on how big your cinnamon roll is, you could easily be at a 3 by the time you get to the last bite.

The trick is to find just the right amount of food for maximum enjoyment with minimum consequences. As an experiment, try rating every bite you eat for awhile to see where that point falls for you.

Holiday and Vacation Eating

Note: If you're in the middle of a tempting situation, use temptation-specific questions such as entitlement, indulgence, or good food eating. Use the following questions if you want to prepare yourself with truth each morning before temptation hits.

1. Do you want to gain, lose, or maintain your weight on this vacation/holiday?
2. What will you need to do to accomplish your goal?
3. Will eating as much as you want make the vacation/holiday more fun? Explain, taking all factors into consideration.
4. What usually happens when you eat as much as you want on holidays and vacations?
5. Do you want that to happen?
6. Will you need to modify your boundaries during this vacation/holiday to make them easier to follow?
7. What do you think would be the most effective boundaries to use?
8. Are boundaries easy to follow, or do you usually have to give up something to follow them?
9. What will have to give up to follow your boundaries this time?
10. What will you gain if you follow your boundaries?
11. When you think of what you'll gain, is it worth the sacrifice?

Bible Verses

Romans 13:14 But put on the Lord Jesus Christ, and make no provision for the flesh in regard to its lusts.

Colossians 3:17 Whatever you do in word or deed, do all in the name of the Lord Jesus, giving thanks through Him to God the Father.

1 Corinthians 6:12 All things are lawful for me, but not all things are profitable. All things are lawful for me, but I will not be mastered by anything.

1 Thessalonians 5:6 So then let us not sleep as others do, but let us be alert and sober.

1 John 2:15-16 Do not love the world not the things in the world. If anyone loves the world, the love of the Father is not in him. For all that is in the world, the lust of the flesh and the lust of the eyes and the boastful pride of life, is not from the Father, but is from the world.

Tips

It's hard to eat well during holidays and vacations because not only are we surrounded by good things to eat, we're also out of our normal routines and often have added stress.

The best way to withstand temptation is to spend extra time renewing your mind before and during the holiday.

If you go on a trip, bring this book along and start each day with a set of questions and Bible verses based on how you think you'll be tempted during the day.

Prepare for holidays by renewing your mind each day the week before the holiday. The more time you spend preparing yourself for temptation, the less chance you'll have of giving in to temptation.

Hopeless Eating

1. How many years have you been struggling with your weight and eating issues?
2. How many years (or weeks) have you been diligent about applying truth to the lies that are fueling your habit?
3. On a scale of 1 to 10, how diligent have you been?
4. When you think of how long you've been renewing your mind compared to how long you've had this problem, is it realistic to expect 100% victory at this point? Why or why not?
5. Since you can't change the past, which of the following do you think God wants you to do now?
   a. Try to find the perfect diet that will make losing weight fun and easy. (Note: does that diet exist?)
   b. Give up and start eating.
   c. Beat yourself up and think about what a loser you are.
   d. Sit back and wait for God to change you in His time.
   e. Remember that you're in a spiritual battle, and expect it to be difficult. Fight the battle with spiritual weapons and renew your mind every time you feel like eating outside your boundaries. Trust God to change you in His time.
6. What should you expect if you choose the last option? (Think of Jesus in the desert, Jesus in Gethsemane, Job's attack by Satan, and Hebrews 12:11.)
7. Is there anything you need to accept?
8. Is there anything you need to do?
9. Would it help to have someone hold you accountable to the renewing of your mind? If so, who could you ask?

Bible verses

Psalm 18:29 For by You I can run upon a troop; and by my God I can leap over a wall.

Psalm 30:5b Weeping may last for the night, but a shout of joy comes in the morning.

Psalm 37:23-24 The steps of a man are established by the Lord, and He delights in his way. When he falls, he will not be hurled headlong, because the Lord is the One who holds his hand.

Jeremiah 32:27 Behold, I am the Lord, the God of all flesh; is anything too difficult for Me?

John 8:10-11 Straightening up, Jesus said to her, "Woman, where are they? Did no one condemn you?" She said, "No one, Lord." And Jesus said, "I do not condemn you, either. Go. From now on sin no more."

Romans 8:1-2 Therefore there is now no condemnation for those who are in Christ Jesus. For the law of the Spirit of life in Christ Jesus has set you free from the law of sin and of death.

Galatians 6:9 Let us not lose heart in doing good, for in due time we will reap if we do not grow weary.

Philippians 1:6 For I am confident of this very thing, that He who began a good work in you will perfect it until the day of Christ Jesus.

Hebrews 10:36 For you have need of endurance, so that when you have done the will of God, you may receive what was promised.

Philippians 3:13-14 Brethren, I do not regard myself as having laid hold of it yet; but one thing I do: forgetting what lies behind and reaching forward to what lies ahead, I press on toward the goal for the prize of the upward call of God in Christ Jesus.

Hebrews 4:15-16 For we do not have a high priest who cannot sympathize with our weaknesses, but One who has been tempted in all things as we are, yet without sin. Therefore let us draw near with confidence to the throne of grace, so that we may receive mercy and find grace to help in time of need.

Hebrews 12:11 All discipline for the moment seems not to be joyful, but sorrowful; yet to those who have been trained by it, afterwards it yields the peaceful fruit of righteousness.

James 1:2-4 Consider it all joy, my brethren, when you encounter various trials, knowing that the testing of your faith produces endurance. And let endurance have its perfect result, that you may be perfect and complete, lacking in nothing.

Tips

Hopeless eating is an attitude that says *I'll never get over this, so why bother?* It usually kicks in after a period of failure.

The key to overcoming hopeless eating is to realize that failure isn't the end of the world. It's just another step on a path that is heading toward victory. Use your failure as an opportunity to go to God and learn from your mistakes.

If you renew your mind every time you break your boundaries, the truth will eventually change you. Not as soon as you'd like, but it will happen eventually. Just keep plugging away and have faith that God will work in you.

For more help with this, read the tips in Tired of the Struggle Eating, Failure, and Perfectionism.

I'll Start Tomorrow Eating

1. What are your boundaries?
2. Is there ever a good (i.e. easy) time to start following your boundaries?
3. What sacrifices will you have to make to lose and/or maintain your weight?
4. Will you have to make those sacrifices no matter when you make the commitment to follow your boundaries?
5. What would you gain by starting to follow your boundaries today?
6. What do you think will happen if you don't start today? Be specific.
7. Would it be better to start following your boundaries today, or is there a good reason to wait?
8. Are you the type of person who can go without boundaries in this area of your life and still lose or maintain your weight? Why or why not?
9. Is there anything you need to accept?
10. What will your life and body look like a couple of months down the road if you develop the habit of consistently following your boundaries?
11. When you think of all you have to gain, is it worth following your boundaries today?

Bible Verses

Romans 6:1-2 What shall we say then? Are we to continue in sin so that grace may increase? May it never be! How shall we who died to sin still live in it?

Romans 13:14 But put on the Lord Jesus Christ, and make no provision for the flesh in regard to its lusts.

Romans 5:3-4 And not only this, but we also exult in our tribulations, knowing that tribulation brings about perseverance; and perseverance, proven character; and proven character, hope.

Hebrews 12:11 All discipline for the moment seems not to be joyful, but sorrowful; yet to those who have been trained by it, afterwards it yields the peaceful fruit of righteousness.

1 Peter 1:14-16 As obedient children, do not be conformed to the former lusts which were yours in your ignorance, but like the Holy One who called you, be holy yourselves also in all your behavior, because it is written, "You shall be holy, for I am holy."

Tips

The best way to break free from I'll Start Tomorrow Eating is to ban that phrase from your vocabulary. Here's why: The minute you say, "I'll start tomorrow," you start feeling noble because you're going to be "so good tomorrow."

And when you feel noble, it's easy to throw caution to the wind and have a wild night of eating. Because after all, you're going to be so good tomorrow!

Try to change your mindset to think of this journey the same way you would think of a marriage. Would you habitually leave your spouse for an all-out day of flirting with other people? Of course not! That wouldn't be good for your relationship.

In like manner, leaving your boundaries for the occasional all-out eating session isn't good for your relationship with food. Make a commitment to follow your boundaries through thick and thin, and it will be harder mentally to have an all-out eating session.

Indulgence Eating

1. Why don't you feel like following your boundaries today?
2. What do you feel like eating?
3. How much would you need to eat before you could honestly say, "That's enough. I don't want any more"? Be specific.
4. At that point would you be:
   a. More satisfied than you are right now.
   b. Less satisfied than you are right now.
   c. About the same as you are right now.
   d. Wishing you could take back the whole eating episode.
5. How often will you follow your boundaries if you only follow them on the days you feel like following them? (Be honest.)
6. What will you gain if you follow your boundaries today, even though it's hard?
7. Do you think God wants you to follow your boundaries? Why or why not?
8. Are boundaries easy to follow or do you usually have to give up something to follow them?
9. What will you have to give up to follow your boundaries this time?
10. When you think of what you'll gain, is it worth the sacrifice?

Bible Verses

Psalm 73:25 Whom have I in heaven but You? And besides You, I desire nothing on earth.

Philippians 1:21 For to me, to live is Christ and to die is gain.

Philippians 3:7 But whatever things were gain to me, those things I have counted as loss for the sake of Christ.

Philippians 4:11-13 Not that I speak from want, for I have learned to be content in whatever circumstances I am. I know how to get along with humble means, and I also know how to live in prosperity; in any and every circumstance I have learned the secret of being filled and going hungry, both of having abundance and suffering need. I can do all things through Him who strengthens me.

Hebrews 12:11 All discipline for the moment seems not to be joyful, but sorrowful; yet to those who have been trained by it, afterwards it yields the peaceful fruit of righteousness.

1 Peter 1:14-16 As obedient children, do not be conformed to the former lusts which were yours in your ignorance, but like the Holy One who called you, be holy yourselves also in all your behavior, because it is written, "You shall be holy, for I am holy."

Tips

Indulgence eating is an attitude that says *I want you, and I'm going to have you. I don't care if you're bad for me, I don't care if you're outside my boundaries, I just want you. And that's enough.*

If we were to apply this same attitude to other things—sex, for example—it would be easier to see that it's a bad attitude. God doesn't want us to have sex with whomever we want whenever we want.

Yet we think it's okay to *eat* whatever we want whenever we want. Why is that?

I'm guessing it's because of the ads we watch on television. Those ads that tell us to indulge ourselves. After all, don't we deserve it? Life is short. We should be enjoying it. And how can we enjoy it without eating what we want?

The key to overcoming indulgence eating is to overcome the attitude that fuels it. Christianity is about loving God with all our heart, soul, and mind—not about loving food with all our heart, soul, and mind.

Sometimes we have to give up things that aren't sinful in and of themselves in order to love God well. I had to do that with sweets. I was writing the chapter on idolatry in *Freedom from Emotional Eating* when it struck me: *Sweets are an idol in my life.*

So I gave them up for a season. For the first time in my life I was willing to go without sweets forever, if necessary. Thankfully, it wasn't necessary. As God broke the control of food on my life, I was able to bring them back in limited quantities until today the only restriction I have on sweets is no dessert before lunch unless it's a fruit-based dessert.

Indulgence eating has a lot in common with entitlement eating, so if these verses and questions don't work, try the entitlement verses and questions.

Justification Eating

1. What do you feel like eating?
2. Will you break a boundary if you eat this?
   a. **Yes:** Which boundary will you break? How were you planning to justify it? Is your justification valid? Why or why not?
   b. **No:** Will you be more likely to break your boundaries later if you eat this now? If so, what are the chances you'll be able to eat this without regretting it later?
3. Are boundaries easy to follow, or do you usually have to give up something to follow them?
4. What will you have to give up to follow your boundaries this time?
5. What will you gain if you follow your boundaries?
6. When you think of what you'll gain, is it worth the sacrifice?

Bible Verses

Romans 13:14 But put on the Lord Jesus Christ, and make no provision for the flesh in regard to its lusts.

1 Corinthians 6:12 All things are lawful for me, but not all things are profitable. All things are lawful for me, but I will not be mastered by anything.

1 Corinthians 10:31 Whether, then, you eat or drink or whatever you do, do all to the glory of God.

1 Thessalonians 5:6 So then let us not sleep as others do, but let us be alert and sober.

1 Thessalonians 5:21 But examine everything carefully; hold fast to that which is good.

James 1:16, 17 Do not be deceived, my beloved brethren. Every good thing given and every perfect gift is from above, coming down from the Father of lights, with whom there is no variation or shifting shadow.

1 Peter 1:14-16 As obedient children, do not be conformed to the former lusts which were yours in your ignorance, but like the Holy One who called you, be holy yourselves also in all your behavior, because it is written, "You shall be holy, for I am holy."

1 Peter 5:8 Be of sober spirit, be on the alert. Your adversary, the devil, prowls around like a roaring lion, seeking someone to devour.

Tips

With justification eating, you tell yourself there's a good reason to break your boundaries. It might be good food, a holiday, a particularly stressful day, a buffet, a potluck, or any number of reasons.

Justification makes it easier to break your boundaries because, after all, there's a good reason to break them.

The key to overcoming justification eating is to realize that your boundaries are there to *protect* you from those times when you feel like you have a good reason to break them.

If you know you're heading into a situation where you'll be tempted to justify the breaking of your boundaries, spend some extra time beforehand renewing your mind to prepare for that temptation.

Perfectionism Eating

1. What are you trying to do perfectly?
2. What would perfection look like in this case? (Give a thorough description.)
3. Are you capable of making that happen? (Be realistic.)
4. Are you simply trying to excel (a good thing) or do you feel like you have to be perfect?
5. Why do you feel like you have to be perfect?
6. Does God think you have to be perfect? Why or why not?
7. Is there anything God wants you to do?
8. Is there anything you need to accept?
9. What can you thank God for in this situation?

Bible verses

Matthew 11:28-30 Come to Me, all who are weary and heavy-laden, and I will give you rest. Take My yoke upon you and learn from Me, for I am gentle and humble in heart, and you will find rest for your souls. For My yoke is easy and My burden is light.

John 8:10-11 Straightening up, Jesus said to her, "Woman, where are they? Did no one condemn you?" She said, "No one, Lord." And Jesus said, "I do not condemn you, either. Go. From now on sin no more."

Ephesians 2:8 For by grace you have been saved through faith; and that not of yourselves, it is the gift of God

Philippians 3:13-14 Brethren, I do not regard myself as having laid hold of it yet; but one thing I do: forgetting what lies behind and reaching forward to what lies ahead, I press on toward the goal for the prize of the upward call of God in Christ Jesus.

Philippians 4:11 Not that I speak from want, for I have learned to be content in whatever circumstances I am.

Hebrews 12:1-2a Therefore, since we have so great a cloud of witnesses surrounding us, let us also lay aside every encumbrance and the sin which so easily entangles us, and let us run with endurance the race that is set before us, fixing our eyes on Jesus, the author and perfecter of faith.

See also: insecurity, regret, stress, and frustration.

Tips

Perfectionism can mess us up in a couple of different ways. First, we beat ourselves up for not having the perfect body. And second, we beat ourselves up for not following our boundaries perfectly.

This is counter-productive! Especially if you tend to eat in response to failure. If you're beating yourself up, try using the self-condemnation questions in the insecurity section as soon as possible.

Also, accept the fact that there is no way you can follow your boundaries perfectly every single day. If you could, you wouldn't be struggling with your weight in the first place!

Accept the fact that some days you'll break your boundaries, and that when you do, you may eat so much that it can undo a whole week's worth of effort in eating well. That's just one of the sad facts of this journey. Try to focus on progress, not perfection.

Procrastination Eating

1. Why do you think it would be a good idea to eat something before you do your job?
2. Based on past experience, what usually happens when you tell yourself you'll do a job later?
3. If you put this off now, when do you think you'll end up doing it? (Be honest.)
4. In the long run, is the procrastination life the good life? Why or why not?
5. If you want to finish this job, will you eventually have to make the sacrifice to work on it?
6. What would you gain by doing it right now?
7. What's the first thing you need to do if you want to work on this job? (Example: Get out your notebook, open the computer file, look up the telephone number, etc.)
8. Why don't you do that right now and see how it goes from there?

Note: If the job seems overwhelming, try breaking it into smaller steps. Each step should be fairly easy and non-intimidating. After breaking it into steps, block the whole project from your mind and focus on one step at a time.

Bible Verses

Psalm 18:29 For by You I can run upon a troop; and by my God I can leap over a wall.

Jeremiah 42:6b Whether it is pleasant or unpleasant, we will listen to the voice of the Lord our God.

2 Corinthians 12:9 And He has said to me, "My grace is sufficient for you, for power is perfected in weakness." Most gladly, therefore, I will rather boast about my weaknesses, so that the power of Christ may dwell in me.

Philippians 4:13 I can do all things through Him who strengthens me.

Philippians 4:19 And my God will supply all your needs according to His riches in glory in Christ Jesus.

Hebrews 10:36 For you have need of endurance, so that when you have done the will of God, you may receive what was promised.

Tips

The best way to stop procrastination eating is to stop procrastinating. I wish I had a five-step plan to overcome it, but I don't. I still struggle with it myself.

This is what God is teaching me: Procrastination is like eating. It doesn't work if you only approach it from a behavioral standpoint. If you want to stop procrastinating, you'll need to change the way you think about work in general.

For example, if I'm thinking life should be easy—and my job is hard—I'm not going to want to do the job no matter how many little tricks I come up with to make myself do it.

It's best if I take the time to work through my self-indulgent attitude first, and then turn to some of the behavioral helps such as dividing the job into manageable steps.

Reward Eating

1. Why do you feel like you deserve a reward?
2. Will you break your boundaries if you reward yourself with food?
   a. **Yes:** If so, which boundary will you break? Is that a good boundary? Why or why not?
   b. **No:** If not, will you be more likely to break your boundaries later if you reward yourself with food now? Why or why not?
3. Can you think of anything else you could reward yourself with besides food? List a few options.
4. What will happen if you continue to reward yourself with food whenever you accomplish something?
5. Do you want that to happen?
6. When you think of the life you want to live, are boundaries a blessing or a curse?
7. What do boundaries add to your life?
8. What will your life and body look like a couple of months down the road if you develop the habit of consistently following your boundaries?
9. When you think of all you'll gain, is it worth the sacrifice?

Bible Verses

Jeremiah 29:11 "For I know the plans I have for you," declares the Lord, "plans for welfare and not for calamity to give you a future and a hope. Then you will call upon Me and come and pray to Me, and I will listen to you. You will seek Me and find Me when you search for Me with all your heart."

Galatians 6:9 Let us not lose heart in doing good, for in due time we will reap if we do not grow weary.

Philippians 4:19 And my God will supply all your needs according to His riches in glory in Christ Jesus.

Colossians 3:1-2 Therefore if you have been raised up with Christ, keep seeking the things above, where Christ is, seated at the right hand of God. Set your mind on the things above, not on the things that are on earth.

James 1:2-4 Consider it all joy, my brethren, when you encounter various trials, knowing that the testing of your faith produces endurance. And let endurance have its perfect result, that you may be perfect and complete, lacking in nothing.

James 1:16, 17 Do not be deceived, my beloved brethren. Every good thing given and every perfect gift is from above, coming down from the Father of lights, with whom there is no variation or shifting shadow.

Tips

The key to gaining victory over reward eating is to realize that breaking the boundaries is *not* a reward. If boundaries make our lives better, than breaking them is a punishment, not a reward.

If you struggle with reward eating, try to find other ways to reward yourself—just be careful those new ways aren't addictive!

Social Eating

If you feel like . . .

1. **People are expecting you to eat:** see living up to expectations or people pleasing.

2. **People will condemn you or get mad at you if you don't eat:** see worry or feeling condemned/rejected.

3. **You have a right to eat because everyone else is eating:** see entitlement eating.

4. **You want to eat because it wouldn't be any fun if you couldn't eat:** see indulgence eating.

Bible Verses

1 Corinthians 13:4-7 Love is patient, love is kind and is not jealous; love does not brag and is not arrogant, does not act unbecomingly; it does not seek its own, is not provoked, does not take into account a wrong suffered, does not rejoice in unrighteousness, but rejoices with the truth; bears all things, believes all things, hopes all things, endures all things.

Philippians 2:4 Do not merely look out for your own personal interests, but also for the interests of others.

Colossians 3:12-15 So, as those who have been chosen of God, holy and beloved, put on a heart of compassion, kindness, humility, gentleness and patience; bearing with one another, and forgiving each other, whoever has a complaint against anyone; just as the Lord forgave you, so also should you. Beyond all these things put on love, which is the perfect bond of unity. Let the peace of Christ rule in your hearts, to which indeed you were called in one body; and be thankful.

1 John 3:16 We know love by this, that He laid down His life for us; and we ought to lay down our lives for the brethren.

Tips

If you're going to a party, try praying through these verses before you go. I used to pray through them on the way to the gathering, while my husband drove. Praying through the verses will help you forget about yourself and focus on loving the people at the party. This will also make it easier to enjoy the party.

Tired of the Struggle Eating

1. Do you ever wish life were easier?
2. Why do you think it's so hard to lose weight and keep it off?
3. What do you usually do when you get discouraged about it?
4. What will happen if you keep doing that?
5. Do you want that to happen?
6. How do you think God feels when He sees you suffering? (Hebrews 4:15)
7. What do you think God wants to do for you in the midst of your struggle? (See Hebrews 4:16 and the other verses below for ideas.)
8. What do you think He wants you to do in the midst of your struggle? (See verses below for ideas.)
9. What will you gain if you go to Him for help with this struggle?
10. When you think of all you'll gain, is it worth taking the time to fight the battle with spiritual weapons?
11. Would it help to have someone hold you accountable to the renewing of your mind? If so, who could you ask?

Bible Verses

Psalm 30:5b Weeping may last for the night, but a shout of joy comes in the morning.

Jeremiah 32:27 Behold, I am the Lord, the God of all flesh; is anything too difficult for Me?

Romans 6:1-2 What shall we say then? Are we to continue in sin so that grace may increase? May it never be! How shall we who died to sin still live in it?

Romans 12:2 And do not be conformed to this world, but be transformed by the renewing of your mind, so that you may prove what the will of God is, that which is good and acceptable and perfect.

Galatians 6:9 Let us not lose heart in doing good, for in due time we will reap if we do not grow weary.

Philippians 1:6 For I am confident of this very thing, that He who began a good work in you will perfect it until the day of Christ Jesus.

Philippians 3:13-14 Brethren, I do not regard myself as having laid hold of it yet; but one thing I do: forgetting what lies behind and reaching forward to what lies ahead, I press on toward the goal for the prize of the upward call of God in Christ Jesus.

Hebrews 4:15-16 For we do not have a high priest who cannot sympathize with our weaknesses, but One who has been tempted in all things as we are, yet without sin. Therefore let us draw near with confidence to the throne of grace, so that we may receive mercy and find grace to help in time of need.

Hebrews 10:36 For you have need of endurance, so that when you have done the will of God, you may receive what was promised.

Hebrews 12:11 All discipline for the moment seems not to be joyful, but sorrowful; yet to those who have been trained by it, afterwards it yields the peaceful fruit of righteousness.

James 1:2-4 Consider it all joy, my brethren, when you encounter various trials, knowing that the testing of your faith produces endurance. And let endurance have its perfect result, that you may be perfect and complete, lacking in nothing.

Tips

Let's face it. It's hard to keep dealing with the same problem over and over. Sometimes we feel like throwing in the towel and just *giving up*.

Don't do it.

Spiritual battles are just what they're called: battles. And battles aren't easy. You can't enter into battle without entering into suffering.

Here's a comforting thought, though. It's far better to suffer *with* God than without Him. Spiritual battles can be intense, sweet times of fellowship with God—so sweet it almost feels like it's worth struggling through the problem just to have those times with God.

I want to encourage you to keep going to Him for help. Renew your mind. Take off those lies and put on the truth. Let the Holy Spirit work in you and minister to you and conform you to His image.

The journey won't be pleasant, but *afterwards*, you'll experience the peaceful fruit of righteousness (Hebrews 12:11). And that will be worth the struggle.

Anger and Annoyance

1. Why are you annoyed? Be specific.
2. Are you surprised by this person's behavior? Why or why not?
3. Why does her behavior bother you so much?
4. Do you think her behavior bothers God? Why or why not?
5. Do you think this person is open to change?
   a. **Yes:** If so, do you think God wants you to talk to her? Why or why not? *
   b. **No:** If not, what will happen if you try to change a person who doesn't want to be changed?
6. How do you think God wants you to respond to this person?
7. What would you need to give up, if anything, to respond the way God wants you to respond?
8. Do you love God (or this person) enough to make that sacrifice?
9. Is there anything you need to accept?
10. What do you think God wants to do for you in the midst of this difficult situation? (See insecurity verses for ideas.)
11. Do you need to add some boundaries to this relationship? If so, what boundaries could you actually enforce? **
12. What can you thank God for in this situation? (Don't forget to include the things you like about this person.)

* **Note:** If you think God wants you to talk to this person, try to renew your mind first so your heart is full of love and respect for her. You'll have a better chance of reaching her if she doesn't feel threatened by your anger or condemnation.

Note: If you're in an abusive or potentially abusive situation, please don't try to handle this situation on your own. Seek help as soon as possible. Also, if you're in an ongoing relationship, it would be helpful to go to a counselor to work out your differences.

Possible things you'll need to accept: that people don't always do what you want them to do, that you don't have the power to change people, that you can't always have what you want, and that life is often unfair.

Possible things you'll need to confess: trying to control people God doesn't want you to control, making something more important than God wants you to make it, hurting others with your anger, and judging and condemning others.

Bible Verses

Matthew 5:43-44, 46 You have heard that it was said, "You shall love your neighbor and hate your enemy." But I say to you, love your enemies and pray for those who persecute you. For if you love those who love you, what reward do you have? Do not even the tax collectors do the same?

Matthew 18:21-22 Then Peter came to Jesus and asked, "Lord, how many times shall I forgive my brother or sister who sins against me? Up to seven times?" Jesus answered, "I tell you, not seven times, but seventy-seven times."

Ephesians 4:26-27 Be angry and yet do not sin; do not let the sun go down on your anger, and do not give the devil an opportunity.

Romans 12:18 If possible, so far as it depends on you, be at peace with all men.

Romans 15:1, 7 Now we who are strong ought to bear the weaknesses of those without strength and not just please ourselves. Each of us is to please his neighbor for his good, to his edification. Therefore, accept one another, just as Christ also accepted us to the glory of God.

1 Corinthians 13:4-5 Love is patient, love is kind and is not jealous; love does not brag and is not arrogant, does not act unbecomingly; it does not seek its own, is not provoked, does not take into account a wrong suffered.

1 Corinthians 13:7 (Love) bears all things, believes all things, hopes all things, endures all things.

Colossians 3:12-15 So, as those who have been chosen of God, holy and beloved, put on a heart of compassion, kindness, humility, gentleness and patience; bearing with one another, and forgiving each other, whoever has a complaint against anyone; just as the Lord forgave you, so also should you. Beyond all these things put on love, which is the perfect bond of unity. Let the peace of Christ rule in your hearts, to which indeed you were called in one body; and be thankful.

Colossians 3:17 Whatever you do in word or deed, do all in the name of the Lord Jesus, giving thanks through Him to God the Father.

1 Peter 1:22 Since you have in obedience to the truth purified your souls for a sincere love of the brethren, fervently love one another from the heart.

1 Peter 3:8-9 To sum up, all of you be harmonious, sympathetic, brotherly, kindhearted, and humble in spirit; not returning evil for evil or insult for insult, but giving a blessing instead; for you were called for the very purpose that you might inherit a blessing.

Note: As you pray through these verses, pray for the person who is bugging you. God will change your heart as you pray for him or her.

See also: discontentment, frustration, insecurity, judgment, pride, and worry.

Discontentment, Boredom, and Loneliness

1. Why are you unhappy (bored or lonely)?
2. What do you think will make you happy?
3. Will that really make you happy? Why or why not?
4. Are you able to create the conditions you think will make you happy?
   a. **Yes:** If so, do you think God wants you to work on that? Why or why not?
   b. **No:** If not, is there anything else you can do to make life better? Explain.
5. Is God enough to satisfy you, even if you don't get what you want?
6. What is one thing you can do to draw closer to Him today?
7. What is one thing you can do to show love to others today? Be specific.
8. Is there anything you need to accept?
9. Is there anything you need to hold with open hands?
10. Is there anything God wants you to do?
11. What can you thank God for in this situation?

Possible things you'll need to accept with boredom: that life isn't always fun and exciting and that sometimes you have to give up fun and excitement to love others well.

Possible things you'll need to accept with loneliness: that people don't always love you the way you want to be loved, that people sometimes leave when you don't want them to leave, that it can be hard to make friends, and that you might have to be the one to make the first move if you want more friends.

Possible things you may need to accept with discontentment: that life doesn't always go the way you want it to go, that people don't always do what you want them to do, that God calls you to love even when it's not easy or fun to love, and that God calls you to be thankful even when you don't feel like being thankful.

Possible things you'll need to confess with boredom, discontentment, and loneliness: that you're making something more important than God wants you to make it, that you're not holding all things with open hands, that you're relying on people and things to get your needs met instead of relying on God, that you're expecting others to reach out to you rather than you reaching out to others, and that you have a demanding spirit.

Bible Verses

Psalm 43:5 Why are you downcast, O my soul? Why so disturbed within me? Put your hope in God, for I will yet praise him, my Savior and my God. NIV

Psalm 40:1-3a I waited patiently for the LORD; he turned to me and heard my cry. He lifted me out of the slimy pit, out of the mud and mire; he set my feet on a rock and gave me a firm place to stand. He put a new song in my mouth, a hymn of praise to our God.

Psalm 63:1 O God, You are my God; I shall seek You earnestly; my soul thirsts for You, my flesh yearns for You, in a dry and weary land where there is so water.

Psalm 63:7-8 When I remember You on my bed, I meditate on You in the night watches, for You have been my help, and in the shadow of Your wings I sing for joy. My soul clings to You; Your right hand upholds me.

Psalm 68:19-20a Blessed be the Lord, who daily bears our burden, the God who is our salvation. God is to us a God of deliverance.

Psalm 73:25 Whom have I in heaven but You? And besides You, I desire nothing on earth.

Jonah 2:9a But I will sacrifice to You with the voice of thanksgiving.

2 Corinthians 4:8-9 We are afflicted in every way, but not crushed; perplexed, but not despairing; persecuted, but not forsaken, struck down, but not destroyed.

John 16:33 These things I (Jesus) have spoken to you, so that in Me you may have peace. In the world you have tribulation, but take courage: I have overcome the world.

Philippians 1:21 For to me, to live is Christ and to die is gain.

Philippians 3:7 But whatever things were gain to me, those things I have counted as loss for the sake of Christ.

Philippians 4:11-13 Not that I speak from want, for I have learned to be content in whatever circumstances I am. I know how to get along with humble means, and I also know how to live in prosperity; in any and every circumstance I have learned the secret of being filled and going hungry, both of having abundance and suffering need. I can do all things through Him who strengthens me.

1 Thessalonians 5:18 In everything give thanks; for this is God's will for you in Christ Jesus.

1 Timothy 6:7-8 For we brought nothing into the world, and we can take nothing out of it. But if we have food and clothing, we will be content with that.

1 John 3:16 We know love by this, that He laid down His life for us; and we ought to lay down our lives for the brethren.

See also: anger, frustration, insecurity, procrastination, and worry.

Envy

1. Why are envious of this person?
2. Are you capable of getting what she has?
   a. **Yes:** If so, what would you have to do to get it? Are you willing to do that? Does God want you to do that? Why or why not?
   b. **No:** If not, do you have blessings that she doesn't have? Explain.
3. Could God give you what she has if He wanted to?
4. Can you think of any reason He might not want to?
5. Is God enough to satisfy you even if you don't get what you want?
6. Is there anything you need to accept?
7. Is there anything you need to confess?
8. What can you thank God for in this situation?

Possible things you'll need to accept: that you don't always get what you want, that you don't always get what others have, that you don't always get what you feel like you deserve, and that life in general isn't fair.

Possible things you'll need to confess: that you're resenting or judging those who have more than you, that you're not being thankful for what you have, that you're not learning how to be content in all situations, and that you're not making life about God.

Bible Verses

Luke 12:15 Then (Jesus) said to them, "Beware, and be on your guard against every form of greed; for not even when one has an abundance does his life consist of possessions."

Philippians 4:11-13 Not that I speak from want, for I have learned to be content in whatever circumstances I am. I know how to get along with humble means, and I also know how to live in prosperity; in any and every circumstance I have learned the secret of being filled and going hungry, both of having abundance and suffering need. I can do all things through Him who strengthens me.

1 Thessalonians 5:18 In everything give thanks; for this is God's will for you in Christ Jesus.

Hebrews 12:1-2a Therefore, since we have so great a cloud of witnesses surrounding us, let us also lay aside every encumbrance and the sin which so easily entangles us, and let us run with endurance the race that is set before us, fixing our eyes on Jesus, the author and perfecter of faith.

1 John 2:15-16 Do not love the world nor the things in the world. If anyone loves the world, the love of the Father is not in him. For all that is in the world, the lust of the flesh and the lust of the eyes and the boastful pride of life, is not from the Father, but is from the world.

See also: anger, discontentment, judgment, and pride.

Frustration

Note: If you're frustrated with something you can't change, turn to the discontentment questions.

1. Why are you frustrated?
2. Based on your past experiences with life (work, relationships, diets, etc.), are you surprised that things aren't going smoothly?
3. Are you expecting life to be easy, or are you accepting the fact that life is often difficult, inefficient, and messy?
4. Are you expecting everyone to co-operate with your plans, or are you remembering that they have their own lives with their own plans?
5. Do you think God wants you to keep working on this project even though it's hard?
   a. **Yes:** If so, what will you need to give up to do what God wants you to do?
   b. **No:** If not, what will you need to give up to do what God wants you to do?
   c. **God doesn't care:** Is this project worth the hassle and effort? Why or why not?
6. Is there anything you need to accept?
7. What can you thank God for in this situation?

Possible things you'll need to accept: that life doesn't always go smoothly, that God often asks us to do hard things, that people don't always cooperate with our plans, and that life is often inefficient, messy, and difficult.

Possible things you'll need to confess: a spoiled rich girl attitude, an unwillingness to work and suffer, a demanding spirit, self-absorption, laziness, judgment, anger, and arrogance.

Bible Verses

John 16:33 These things I (Jesus) have spoken to you, so that in Me you may have peace. In the world you have tribulation, but take courage: I have overcome the world.

2 Corinthians 4:8-10 We are afflicted in every way, but not crushed; perplexed, but not despairing; persecuted, but not forsaken; struck down, but not destroyed; always carrying about in the body the dying of Jesus, so that the life of Jesus also may be manifested in our body.

2 Corinthians 4:16-17 Therefore we do not lose heart, but though our outer man is decaying, yet our inner man is being renewed day by day. For momentary, light affliction is producing for us an eternal weight of glory far beyond all comparison.

2 Corinthians 10:3-5 For though we walk in the flesh, we do not war according to the flesh, for the weapons of our warfare are not of the flesh, but divinely powerful for the destruction of fortresses. We are destroying speculations and every lofty thing raised up against the knowledge of God, and we are taking every thought captive to the obedience of Christ.

Ephesians 6:10-11 Finally, be strong in the Lord and in the strength of His might. Put on the full armor of God, so that you will be able to stand firm against the schemes of the devil.

Philippians 1:6 For I am confident of this very thing, that He who began a good work in you will perfect it until the day of Christ Jesus.

Philippians 4:11-13 Not that I speak from want, for I have learned to be content in whatever circumstances I am. I know how to get along with humble means, and I also know how to live in prosperity; in any and every circumstance I have learned the secret of being filled and going hungry, both of having abundance and suffering need. I can do all things through Him who strengthens me.

Hebrews 4:15-16 For we do not have a high priest who cannot sympathize with our weaknesses, but One who has been tempted in all things as we are, yet without sin. Therefore let us draw near with confidence to the throne of grace, so that we may receive mercy and find grace to help in time of need.

Hebrews 12:11 All discipline for the moment seems not to be joyful, but sorrowful; yet to those who have been trained by it, afterwards it yields the peaceful fruit of righteousness.

1 John 4:4b Greater is He who is within you than he who is in the world.

See also: anger, discontentment, and perfectionism.

Greed and Lust

1. What is it that you want? Be specific.
2. Why do you want that?
3. Do you think God wants that? If not, what does He want ?
4. Are God's priorities different than your priorities? Explain.
5. What will happen if you clutch too tightly to what you want?
6. Do you want that to happen? If not, what will you need to do to protect yourself?
7. What will you your life look like a few months down the road if you renew your mind every time this situation comes up?
8. What will your life look like if you indulge yourself every time the situation comes up?
9. Is there anything you need to accept?
10. Is there anything you need to do?

Possible things you'll need to accept: that greed and lust really are sins, that they hurt your relationship with God and often with other people, and that you'll never get enough to satisfy you if you're trying to fill yourself up with anything other than God.

Possible things you'll need to confess: making an idol of whatever it is that you want, impure motives and thoughts, not loving God with all your heart, soul, and mind, and not loving your neighbor as yourself.

Bible Verses

Jeremiah 2:13 For My people have committed two evils: they have forsaken Me, the fountain of living waters, to hew for themselves cisterns, broken cisterns that can hold no water.

Luke 12:15 Then (Jesus) said to them, "Beware, and be on your guard against every form of greed; for not even when one has an abundance does his life consist of possessions."

Romans 13:14 But put on the Lord Jesus Christ, and make no provision for the flesh in regard to its lusts.

1 Corinthians 6:12 All things are lawful for me, but not all things are profitable. All things are lawful for me, but I will not be mastered by anything.

Philippians 3:7 But whatever things were gain to me, those things I have counted as loss for the sake of Christ.

Philippians 4:11 Not that I speak from want, for I have learned to be content in whatever circumstances I am.

Colossians 3:5 Therefore consider the members of your earthly body as dead to immorality, impurity, passion, evil desire, and greed, which amounts to idolatry.

Hebrews 12:1-2a Therefore, since we have so great a cloud of witnesses surrounding us, let us also lay aside every encumbrance and the sin which so easily entangles us, and let us run with endurance the race that is set before us, fixing our eyes on Jesus, the author and perfecter of faith.

See also: discontentment and envy.

Insecurity Bible Verses

Psalm 3:3 But You, O Lord, are a shield about me, my glory, and the One who lifts my head.

Psalm 27:1b, 5 The Lord is the defense of my life; whom shall I dread? For in the day of trouble He will conceal me in His tabernacle; He will lift me up on a rock.

Psalm 37:23-24 The steps of a man are established by the Lord, and He delights in his way. When he falls, he will not be hurled headlong, because the Lord is the One who holds his hand.

Psalm 91:2-4 I will say to the Lord, "My refuge and my fortress, my God in whom I trust!" For it is He who delivers you from the snare of the trapper and from the deadly pestilence. He will cover you with His pinions, and under His wings you may seek refuge; His faithfulness is a shield and bulwark.

Psalm 139:13-15 For You formed my inward parts; You wove me in my mother's womb. I will give thanks to You, for I am fearfully and wonderfully made; Wonderful are Your works, And my soul knows it very well. My frame was not hidden from You when I was made in secret, and skillfully wrought in the depths of the earth.

Psalm 147:2-3 The Lord builds up Jerusalem; He gathers the outcasts of Israel. He heals the brokenhearted and binds up their wounds.

Isaiah 62:4a, 5b It will no longer be said to you, "Forsaken," Nor to your land will it any longer be said, "Desolate"; But you will be called, "My delight is in her," And your land, "Married";

for the Lord delights in you, and as the bridegroom rejoices over the bride, so your God will rejoice over you.

Jeremiah 31:20 "Is Ephraim My dear son? Is he a delightful child? Indeed, as often as I have spoken against him, I certainly still remember him; Therefore My heart yearns for him; I will surely have mercy on him," declares the Lord.

Jeremiah 31:3-4 The Lord appeared to him from afar, saying, "I have loved you with an everlasting love; therefore I have drawn you with lovingkindness. Again I will build you and you will be rebuilt, O virgin of Israel! Again you will take up your tambourines, and go forth to the dances of the merrymakers.

Zephaniah 3:17 The Lord your God is in your midst, a victorious warrior. He will exult over you with joy, He will be quiet in His love, He will rejoice over you with shouts of joy.

Zechariah 2:10 Sing for joy and be glad, O daughter of Zion; for behold I am coming and I will dwell in your midst.

Romans 3:23 For all have sinned and fall short of the glory of God.

Romans 5:8 But God demonstrates His own love toward us, in that while we were yet sinners, Christ died for us.

Galatians 1:10 For am I now seeking the favor of men, or of God? Or am I striving to please men? If I were still trying to please men, I would not be a bond-servant of Christ.

Ephesians 2:10 For we are His workmanship, created in Christ Jesus for good works, which God prepared beforehand so that we would walk in them.

Romans 8:1 Therefore there is now no condemnation for those who are in Christ Jesus.

Philippians 1:6 For I am confident of this very thing, that He who began a good work in you will perfect it until the day of Christ Jesus.

Romans 8:35, 38-39 Who will separate us from the love of Christ? Will tribulation, or distress, or persecution, or famine, or nakedness, or peril, or sword? For I am convinced that neither death, nor life, nor angels, nor principalities, nor things present, nor things to come, nor powers, nor height, nor depth, nor any other created thing, will be able to separate us from the love of God, which is in Christ Jesus our Lord.

2 Corinthians 5:9 Therefore we also have as our ambition, whether at home or absent, to be pleasing to Him.

1 Peter 2:9 But you are a chosen race, a royal priesthood, a holy nation, a people for God's own possession, so that you may proclaim the excellencies of Him who has called you out of darkness into His marvelous light.

See also: regret, discontentment, worry, and self-condemnation.

Tips

When you pray these Scriptures, picture God doing the things these verses talk about. Imagine Him reaching down to grab hold of your hand when you've said something dumb. Or lifting you up on a rock to protect you when life is difficult. Or smiling at you as He flings out His arms and says, "Come here, you delightful child."

As you picture God in these roles, my prayer is that you'll feel treasured, cherished, and accepted by your Father who knows your every sin, yet still delights in you.

Insecurity: Feeling Inadequate

1. Why do you think you're inadequate?
2. What do you think you have to do or have to be acceptable?
3. Are you capable of making that happen right now?
4. What do you look like when you see yourself through the eyes of the world and/or the eyes of your own expectations?
5. Is that how God sees you?
6. Who are you in God's eyes, and how does He feel about you? (Look at the insecurity verses for ideas.)
7. How is God's view of you different than your own view or the world's view?
8. If the Living God, King of the Universe, says you're acceptable, does anyone else, including you, have the right to say you're unacceptable?
9. Is God's love enough to satisfy you even if you're not the person you want to be?
10. What can you thank God for in this situation?

Note: If you're feeling inadequate because of sin, then God wants you to address your sin and work on being transformed through the renewing of your mind (Hebrews 12, Romans 12:1-2). But He's a loving God who wants to help you, not a condemning God who wants to beat you up (Hosea, Romans 8:1, Revelations 12:10, Insecurity Verses).

Possible things you'll need to accept: that you'll never be as good as you want to be, that you can't hide your faults and sins from others, and that you can't live life without messing up at times. Fortunately, everyone else in the world is in the same boat, and God is enough to make up for our shortcomings!

Possible things you'll need to confess: caring more about becoming a perfect person than about loving God and others well, caring more about getting others to love and accept you than about getting yourself to love and accept others, and spending so much time trying to be acceptable in the world's eyes that you don't have time to spend with God.

See also: discontentment, self-condemnation, and regret.

Insecurity: Feeling Rejected or Condemned

1. Is it possible to live life without ever being rejected or condemned?
2. What did this person do to make you feel rejected or condemned? Be specific.
3. Does this person do that sort of thing with other people, or does he only do it with you? (If he only does it with you, why do you think he only does it with you?)
4. Do you think his behavior is a sign that he doesn't love or respect you in particular, or is this just an example of the way he responds to people in general?
5. Did you do anything to make this person reject you or condemn you? If so, what did you do? (If not, skip to #7)
6. Do you think God wanted you to do that? Explain.
   a. **Yes:** If so, are you willing to be rejected and condemned for God?
   b. **No:** If not, what do you think God wants you to do now, given the fact that you can't change what's already been done? (For example: apologize, make restitution, let it go, try to change, etc.)
   c. **Not sure:** Was your action loving? If not, was there a good (biblically good) reason for doing it, keeping 1 Corinthians 13 in mind?
   d. **God doesn't care:** Would you rather have this person like you and accept you, or would you rather keep doing what you're doing? (Remember, you can't control the other person.)
7. Is there anything you need to accept about this person and

the way he handles relationships? *

8. Is God's love enough to satisfy you even if this person rejects or condemns you?

9. What do you think God wants to do for you in the midst of this difficult situation? (See insecurity verses and Hebrews 12:11 for ideas.)

10. Who are you in God's eyes and how does He feel about you? (Spend some time on this one.)

11. How do you think God wants you to respond to this person who is condemning or rejecting you? *

12. Is there anything you need to accept?

13. What can you thank God for in this situation?

* Note: If this person is treating you with disrespect, you may need to put up some boundaries. If this person is abusive, please get professional help as soon as possible.

Possible things you'll need to accept: that you can't make everyone love and respect you no matter how hard you try, that you're not always easy to love and respect (none of us are), that if people are going to love and respect you, they'll have to love and respect the real and imperfect you, and that no one except God is capable of loving and accepting you perfectly.

Possible things you'll need to confess: any sins you committed that made this person reject or condemn you, rejecting or condemning them in retaliation, focusing more on getting others to love and respect you rather than on getting yourself to love and respect others, and neglecting your responsibilities in order to avoid making someone mad.

See also: discontentment, judgment, feeling inadequate, people pleasing, and worry.

Insecurity: Living Up to Expectations

1. What does this person want you to do?
2. Are you capable of doing what she wants you to do?
3. Why do you feel like you need to live up to her expectations?
4. Is that a good reason to do what this person wants you to do? Why or why not?
5. Do you think it's possible to love this person well if you're always trying to live up to her expectations? Why or why not?
6. How would you handle this situation if you didn't have to worry about disappointing this person? Why would you handle it that way?
7. How do you think God wants you to handle this situation?
8. Why do you think He wants you to handle it that way?
9. Is there anything you need to give up to do what God wants you to do?
10. Is there anything you need to accept?

Note: If you're having a hard time making a decision, look for the decision making questions at my blog. The post is called Decision Making and God's Will: 13 Questions To Help.

Possible things you'll need to accept: that you can't make everyone happy no matter how hard you try, that you can't always know what's best, that some people will get mad at you if you tell them no, and that sometimes you need to tell them no.

Possible things you'll need to confess: basing your decisions on what others want you to do rather than on what God wants you to do, neglecting your other responsibilities in order to avoid making someone mad, doing things out of self-protection rather than out of love for God and others, doing things grudgingly rather than with a whole heart, and making an idol of other people's opinions of you.

See also: anger, discontentment, feeling condemned and rejected, people pleasing, frustration, and worry.

Insecurity: People Pleasing

Note: Use the "Living Up to Expectations" questions if someone is asking or expecting you to do something.

1. Why do you want to make this person happy?
2. What will make him happy?
3. Are you able to make that happen?
4. Will that really make him happy? Explain.
5. Are you:
    a. Interfering with what God wants to do in this person's life by always trying to make him happy? Explain.
    b. Tempted to do something God doesn't want you to do (or not do something God wants you to do) just so you can make this person happy? Explain.
    c. Remembering that only God can fill this person up and make him happy?
    d. Neglecting your responsibilities (as a parent, for example) just to avoid making this person mad?
6. How do you think God wants you to handle this situation?
7. Why do you think He wants you to handle it that way?
8. What would you need to sacrifice, give up, or risk to do what God wants you to do?
9. What will you gain if you do what God wants you to do?
10. Is there anything you need to accept?
11. What can you thank God for in this situation?

Possible things you'll need to accept: that you can't make everyone happy no matter how hard you try, that sometimes people are unhappy and there's nothing you can do about it, and that sometimes God actually wants you to do things that will make others unhappy. It's also good to remember that just because people are unhappy, it doesn't mean they don't love you. More often than not, it just means they're unhappy.

Possible things you'll need to confess: making an idol of avoiding conflict or getting everyone to like you, neglecting your responsibilities in order to make everyone happy, making life so easy for others that they never have an opportunity to learn to rely on God, and caring more about what others think than what God thinks.

See also: living up to expectations, greed/lust, worry, and feeling inadequate.

Insecurity: Self-Condemnation

1. Why do you think you're a failure (terrible person, bad Christian, etc.)?
2. Does that really make you a failure (terrible person/bad Christian, etc.)? Why or why not? *
3. Whose standards are you using to determine whether or not you're acceptable?
4. What does God think of those standards?
5. How does God feel about you? (See insecurity verses for ideas.)
6. God is not a condemning perfectionist parent. He's a loving Father who says, "Come to me, my beloved, and let me help." In what areas do you need help?
7. Take some time to ask Him to help you with those areas.
8. Is there anything you need to accept?
9. Is there anything God wants you to do?
10. What can you thank God for in this situation?

* If you're having a hard time answering this question, look through the insecurity verses and think about grace. If you're going the bad Christian route, think about the life of David and Romans 3:23.

Possible things you'll need to accept: that you'll never be as good as you want to be, that others will see your imperfections (just as you see their imperfections), and that you'll fail at times. Everyone does—it's part of the human condition, so you might as well get used to it!

Possible things you'll need to confess: condemning someone God loves (you!), giving yourself permission to give up because you feel like a failure, and making "success" more important than God wants you to make it.

See also: feeling inadequate, discontentment, envy, greed/lust, worry, and anger.

Insecurity: Social Situations

1. Why do the people at this gathering intimidate you?
2. If the people at the gathering don't appear to like or respect you, does that automatically mean they don't? What else could it mean?
3. Do you think God wants you to reach out to these people even though you risk rejection? Why or why not? *
4. What attitude does He want you to have? (Philippians 2:3-8)
5. How does God want you to treat the people at this gathering? (1 Corinthians 13:4-8)
6. Is there anything you need to give up to love these people well? Explain.
7. Is there anything you need to accept?
8. What can you thank God for in this situation?

* **Note:** There may be situations when the answer to this question is no. The key is to base your actions on what God wants you to do, not on what you feel comfortable doing. Also, you'll have to accept the sad fact that just because you're willing to reach out to others, that doesn't mean they'll want to reach out back.

Possible things you'll need to accept: that you can't live life without saying and doing dumb things at times, that not all social situations will be comfortable, that you'll never be as perfect as you want to be, that you'll never be as popular as you want to be, and that if people are going to love and respect you, they'll have to love and respect the imperfect and sometimes unpopular you.

Possible things you'll need to confess: caring more about what others think than what God thinks, caring more about getting others to love you than about getting yourself to love others, doing things God doesn't want you to do in order to be popular, and an unwillingness to be uncomfortable and take risks to love others well.

See also: discontentment, worry, feeling inadequate, and envy.

Bible Verses

1 Corinthians 13:4-8a Love is patient, love is kind. It does not envy, it does not boast, it is not proud. It does not dishonor others, it is not self-seeking, it is not easily angered, it keeps no record of wrongs. Love does not delight in evil but rejoices with the truth. It always protects, always trusts, always hopes, always perseveres. Love never fails.

Philippians 2:4 Do not merely look out for your own personal interests, but also for the interests of others.

1 John 3:16 We know love by this, that He laid down His life for us; and we ought to lay down our lives for the brethren.

See also: discontentment, other insecurity questions, worry, and insecurity Bible verses.

Judgment

1. Is what you're judging a sin or just a different way of doing things?

2. If it's a difference:

    a. Does God want you to make your own standards a law for others to follow?

    b. Are you willing to accept another way of doing things?

3. If it's a sin:

    a. Are you grieving over this person's sin, or are you condemning him for it?

    b. Is your desire to bring this person back to God, or are you more concerned with how his behavior is affecting your life (either directly or indirectly)?

    c. How can you best help this person?

4. How do you compare to the person you're judging? Are you judging from a position of strength or weakness?

    a. If strength to weakness:

    - If you've never struggled with this weakness: Do you realize how blessed you are to never have struggled with it ?

    - If you've overcome this weakness: Are you thanking God for giving you the strength and desire to overcome it, or are you beginning to believe that it was all your own doing?

    b. If weakness to weakness:

    - Why are you condemning it in someone else when you know how hard it is to overcome?

    c. If weakness to strength:

    - Does this strong person deserve your judgment just because you're weak in this area?

5. Is this person's sin or fault worse than your own sin of condemning him?
6. How do you think God wants you to respond to this person?
7. Is there anything you need to accept?
8. Is there anything you need to confess?
9. What can you thank God for in this situation?

Possible things you'll need to accept: that people do wrong things, that sometimes they get away with the wrong things they do, that your way isn't always the best way or the only way, and that you're not in control.

Possible things you'll need to confess: acting like God when you're not God, turning your own standards into a law for others to follow, caring too much about things God doesn't care about (such as appearance and status), arrogance, pride, and resentment.

Bible Verses

Matthew 7:3-5 Why do you look at the speck that is in your brother's eye, but do not notice the log that is in your own eye? Or how can you say to your brother, 'Let me take the speck out of your eye,' and behold, the log is in your own eye? You hypocrite, first take the log out of your own eye, and then you will see clearly to take the speck out of your brother's eye.

John 3:17 For God did not send the Son into the world to judge the world, but that the world might be saved through Him.

Romans 2:4 Or do you think lightly of the riches of His kindness and tolerance and patience, not knowing that the kindness of God leads you to repentance?

Romans 14:4 Who are you to judge the servant of another? To his own master he stands or falls; and he will stand, for the Lord is able to make him stand.

Romans 14:13 Therefore let us not judge one another anymore, but rather determine this—not to put an obstacle or a stumbling block in a brother's way.

James 4:6 But He gives a greater grace. Therefore it says, "God is opposed to the proud, but gives grace to the humble."

James 4:11-12 Do not speak against one another, brethren He who speaks against a brother or judges his brother, speaks against the law and judges the law; but if you judge the law, you are not a doer of the law but a judge of it. There is only one Lawgiver and Judge, the One who is able to save and to destroy; but who are you who judge your neighbor?

See also: anger, envy, insecurity, and pride.

Pride

1. Why do you think you're a better person/Christian than this person?
2. Does God think you're better? If not, what does He think?
3. How does putting yourself "above" this person affect your relationship with God and your relationship with this person?
4. Are you remembering that God gave you everything you have, or are you beginning to think it's all your own doing?
5. What has God blessed you with?
6. How does He want you to use those blessings?
7. Is there anything you need to confess?
8. What can you be thankful for in this situation?

Possible things you'll need to accept: that you're not as great as you think you are, that you're not better than others, and that God has given you everything you have.

Possible things you'll need to confess: making more of yourself than you have a right to make, an unwillingness to change, an unwillingness to look at your own sin, an unwillingness to serve others, and a failure to recognize that God is the one who is responsible for your strengths, not you.

Bible Verses

Exodus 3:5 Then He said, "Do not come near here; remove your sandals from your feet, for the place on which you are standing is holy ground."

Deuteronomy 8:17-18a You may say to yourself, "My power and the strength of my hands have produced this wealth for me." But remember the Lord your God, for it is He who gives you the ability to produce wealth. NIV

Psalm 100:3 Know that the Lord Himself is God. It is He who has made us, and not we ourselves; we are His people and the sheep of His pasture.

Psalm 138:6 Though the Lord is high, he looks upon the lowly, but the proud he knows from afar. NIV

1 Corinthians 4:7 For who regards you as superior? What do you have that you did not receive? And if you did receive it, why do you boast as if you had not received it?

2 Corinthians 3:5 Not that we are adequate in ourselves to consider anything as coming from ourselves, but our adequacy is from God.

1 Peter 5:5b Clothe yourselves with humility toward one another, for God is opposed to the proud, but gives grace to the humble

1 Peter 5:6 Therefore humble yourselves under the mighty hand of God, that He may exalt you at the proper time.

See also: anger, envy, and judgment.

Regret

1. What do you wish you would have done or not done?
2. Do you think God wishes you had done things differently? Why or why not?
3. Since you can't go back and change what you did or didn't do, how do you think God wants you to respond now?
4. How would Satan like you to respond?
5. What can you gain from this experience if you respond the way God wants you to respond?
6. Can God redeem this situation even if you really messed up? Explain.
7. Is there anything you need to accept?
8. Is there anything you need to confess?
9. Do you need to apologize to anyone or make restitution?
10. What can you thank God for in this situation?

Possible things you'll need to accept: that you can't go back and change what you did in the past, that your actions sometimes hurt others, that you can't fix everything in life, that you may need to live with the consequences of your actions, and that sometimes you'll make bad choices in life—everyone does. Just remember, God can redeem anything.

Possible things you'll need to confess: not doing something God wanted you to do, doing something God didn't want you to do, and making something more important than God wants you to make it.

Bible Verses

Proverbs 3:5-6 Trust in the Lord with all your heart and do not lean on your own understanding. In all your ways acknowledge Him, and He will make your paths straight.

Jeremiah 29:11 "For I know the plans I have for you," declares the Lord, "plans for welfare and not for calamity to give you a future and a hope."

Jeremiah 32:27 Behold, I am the Lord, the God of all flesh; is anything too difficult for Me?

John 8:10-11 Straightening up, Jesus said to her, "Woman, where are they? Did no one condemn you?" She said, "No one, Lord." And Jesus said, "I do not condemn you, either. Go. From now on sin no more."

Philippians 3:13-14 Brethren, I do not regard myself as having laid hold of it yet; but one thing I do: forgetting what lies behind and reaching forward to what lies ahead, I press on toward the goal for the prize of the upward call of God in Christ Jesus.

Romans 8:28 And we know that God causes all things to work together for good to those who love God, to those who are called according to His purpose.

Romans 8:1-2 Therefore there is now no condemnation for those who are in Christ Jesus. For the law of the Spirit of life in Christ Jesus has set you free from the law of sin and of death.

Philippians 4:11b-13 I have learned to be content whatever the circumstances. I know what it is to be in need, and I know what it is to have plenty. I have learned the secret of being content in any and every situation, whether well fed or hungry, whether living in plenty or in want. I can do all things through Him who strengthens me.

1 Thessalonians 5:18 In everything give thanks; for this is God's will for you in Christ Jesus.

1 John 1:9 If we confess our sins, He is faithful and righteous to forgive us our sins and to cleanse us from all unrighteousness.

See also: anger, discontentment, envy, perfectionism, and worry.

Stress: Beginning of Work Day

1. Why are you so stressed today?
2. Can you make a list of all the things you need to get done? If so, go ahead and do that.
3. Are you able to accomplish everything on your list today?
   a. **Yes:** If so, why are you feeling so stressed? Consider doing a different set of questions depending on your answer to this question.
   b. **No:** Is there anything you need to accept?
4. Of all the things on your list:
   a. What two things are you dreading the most? Why are you dreading them?
   b. What two things are the most important?
   c. Is there anything you absolutely need to get done today?
   d. Is there anything God wants you to do today that's not even on your list?
5. Looking back over your answers to the last question, make a prioritized, realistic list for the day. If you have problems following the list, turn to the procrastination questions.
6. How can you love God and others best as you work on your list today?
7. If life is about loving God and others, will it be the end of the world if you don't finish your list today?

Possible things you'll need to accept: that you might not be able to get everything done, that you might not have time to do it as well as you want to do it, and that sometimes life is busy and there's nothing you can do about it.

Possible things you'll need to confess: making recreation, work, projects, or hobbies more important than God wants you to make them, being so busy you don't have time for God, and hurting others in your quest to get things done.

Bible Verses

Psalm 18:29 For by You I can run upon a troop; and by my God I can leap over a wall.

Psalm 18:34 He trains my hands for battle so that my arms can bend a bow of bronze.

Psalm 61:2-4 From the end of the earth I call to You when my heart is faint; lead me to the rock that is higher than I. For You have been a refuge for me, a tower of strength against the enemy. Let me dwell in your tent forever; let me take refuge in the shelter of Your wings.

Isaiah 40:31 Yet those who wait for the Lord will gain new strength; they will mount up with wings like eagles, they will run and not get tired, they will walk and not become weary.

Jeremiah 29:11-13 "For I know the plans I have for you," declares the Lord, "plans for welfare and not for calamity to give you a future and a hope. Then you will call upon Me and come and pray to Me, and I will listen to you. You will seek Me and find Me when you search for Me with all your heart."

Jeremiah 32:27 Behold, I am the Lord, the God of all flesh; is anything too difficult for Me?

Jeremiah 42:6b Whether it is pleasant or unpleasant, we will listen to the voice of the Lord our God.

Lamentations 3:22-23 The Lord's lovingkindnesses indeed never cease, for his compassions never fail. They are new every morning; great is Your faithfulness.

Matthew 11:28 Come to Me, all who are weary and heavy-laden, and I will give you rest.

Luke 10:41-42 But the Lord answered and said to her, "Martha, Martha, you are worried and bothered about so many things; but only one thing is necessary, for Mary has chosen the good part, which shall not be taken away from her."

2 Corinthians 12:9 And He has said to me, "My grace is sufficient for you, for power is perfected in weakness." Most gladly, therefore, I will rather boast about my weaknesses, so that the power of Christ may dwell in me.

Philippians 4:13 I can do all things through Him who strengthens me.

See also: insecurity, procrastination, perfectionism, and worry.

Stress: End of the Work Day

Why are you so stressed right now? Be specific. Renew your mind, using the list below as a guide.

If you're stressed because:

1. **You can't stop thinking about all you have to do:** see self-condemnation, greed/lust (what you want is a finished to-do list), worry, or end of day stress on the next page.
2. **You're worried about what people will think if don't perform well:** see people pleasing, worry, or living up to expectations.
3. **You didn't get enough done today:** see regret, self-condemnation, or end of the day stress on next page.
4. **You feel like you have to be perfect:** see perfectionism or end of work day stress.
5. **You don't want to do anything else after such a long day:** see discontentment.
6. **You don't think you should *have* to do anything else after such a long day:** see entitlement.
7. **You're frustrated that life is so hard:** see frustration or tired of the struggle eating (adapt the questions to your current struggle).
8. **You said or did something dumb today**: see regret.
9. **You're worried or annoyed**: see worry or anger.

Possible things you'll need to accept: that life is busy sometimes, that you're not perfect, that you're not in control, that sometimes you'll look back on your day and think, *I didn't get even one thing done*, and that sometimes you won't get everything done even if you work hard all day.

Possible things you'll need to confess: making an idol of your to-do list, work, hobbies, recreation, and/or free time, being so consumed by your to-do list that you don't have time for God and others, making life about things other than God, and hurting others in your quest to get things done.

End of Work Day Stress Questions

1. What did you accomplish today? (Be specific.)
2. Were you able to complete everything on your list?
   a. **Yes:** If so, why are you still feeling stressed?
   b. **No:** If not, what didn't you finish, and why didn't you finish it? (Be specific.)
3. Are you being realistic about how much you can accomplish each day?
4. Is there anything you need to change about the way you do things tomorrow?
5. Are you remembering that life is about loving God and others? If not, what are you thinking life is about?
6. Since you can't change what's been done or not done, what do you think God wants you to do now?
   a. Keep working in a frenzy, knowing that it's essential to finish your list.
   b. Keep working in peace, knowing that life is about God, not your list.
   c. Quit working, but spend the rest of the night thinking about what you didn't get done.
   d. Quit working, forget about the list, and remember that life is about God, not your list.
7. Why do you think He wants you to do that?
8. Is there anything you need to trust Him with?
9. Is there anything you need to accept?
10. What do you think God wants to teach you from this trial?
11. What will you need to do if you want to learn the lesson He has for you? (See also John 15:4-5, Romans 12:2.)

Bible Verses

Psalm 46:10 Cease striving and know that I am God; I will be exalted among the nations, I will be exalted in the earth.

Psalm 63:7-8 When I remember You on my bed, I meditate on You in the night watches, for You have been my help, and in the shadow of Your wings I sing for joy. My soul clings to You; Your right hand upholds me.

Isaiah 12:2 Behold, God is my salvation, I will trust and not be afraid. For the Lord God is my strength and my song, and He has become my salvation.

Isaiah 26:3 The steadfast of mind You will keep in perfect peace, because he trusts in you.

Jeremiah 32:27 Behold, I am the Lord, the God of all flesh; is anything too difficult for me?

Jeremiah 32:17 Ah Lord God! Behold, You have made the heavens and the earth by Your great power and by your outstretched arm! Nothing is too difficult for you.

Matthew 6:24 "No one can serve two masters; for either he will hate the one and love the other, or he will be devoted to one and despise the other. You cannot serve God and wealth.

Matthew 11:28-30 Come to Me, all who are weary and heavy-laden, and I will give you rest. Take My yoke upon you and learn from Me, for I am gentle and humble in heart, and you will find rest for your souls. For My yoke is easy and My burden is light.

Luke 10:41-42 But the Lord answered and said to her, "Martha, Martha, you are worried and bothered about so many things; but only one thing is necessary, for Mary has chosen the good part, which shall not be taken away from her."

John 14:27 Peace I leave with you; My peace I give to you; not as the world gives do I give to you. Do not let your heart be troubled, nor let it be fearful.

John 15:4-5 Abide in Me, and I in you. As the branch cannot bear fruit of itself unless it abides in the vine, so neither *can* you unless you abide in Me. I am the vine, you are the branches; he who abides in Me and I in him, he bears much fruit, for apart from Me you can do nothing.

2 Corinthians 12:9 And He has said to me, "My grace is sufficient for you, for power is perfected in weakness." Most gladly, therefore, I will rather boast about my weaknesses, so that the power of Christ may dwell in me.

Hebrews 12:11 All discipline for the moment seems not to be joyful, but sorrowful; yet to those who have been trained by it, afterwards it yields the peaceful fruit of righteousness.

James 4:13-15 Come now, you who say, "Today or tomorrow we will go to such and such a city, and spend a year there and engage in business and make a profit." Yet you do not know what your life will be like tomorrow. You are just a vapor that appears for a little while and then vanishes away. Instead, you ought to say, "If the Lord wills, we will live and also do this or that."

Worry

1. What are you worried about? Be specific.
2. What are the odds that your worry will take place?
3. What do you hope will happen? Be specific.
   a. Why do you want that to happen?
   b. Do you think God wants the same thing you want? Why or why not?
4. Are God's priorities different than your priorities in this situation? If so, how are they different?
5. Can you control this situation? Why or why not?
6. If not, what will you need to accept right from the beginning?
7. Can you influence this situation?
   a. **Yes:** If so, what could you do? Do you think God wants you to do that? Why or why not?
   b. **No:** If not, have you accepted the fact that there's nothing you can do to keep your worry from taking place?
8. Are you willing to trust God for the things you can't control?
9. Is God worthy of your trust? Why or why not?
10. What do you think God wants to do for you (and/or your loved ones) in this situation? (See the insecurity Bible verses and Romans 5:3-5 for ideas.)
11. How can you love God and others best in this situation?
12. What can you thank God for in this situation?

Note: If you're having a hard time thinking of things to be thankful for, try meditating on the attributes of God. Thank Him for who He is (all-knowing, all-powerful, all-loving, just, merciful, compassionate, etc.) and why that makes a difference in this situation.

Possible things you'll need to accept: that the unthinkable will happen, that you're not in control, that there's often nothing you can do to prevent bad things from happening, and that you might not get what you want.

Possible things you'll need to confess: making idols of people or things, trying to control things God doesn't want you to control, and a lack of trust in God.

Bible Verses

Psalm 27:1, 3 The Lord is my light and my salvation; whom shall I fear? Though a host encamp against me, my heart will not fear; though war arise against me, in spite of this I shall be confident.

Psalm 27:5 For in the day of trouble He will conceal me in His tabernacle; In the secret place of His tent He will hide me; He will lift me up on a rock.

Psalm 27:13 I would have despaired unless I had believed that I would see the goodness of the Lord in the land of the living.

Psalm 46:1-2, 7 God is our refuge and strength, a very present help in trouble. Therefore we will not fear, though the earth should change and though the mountains slip into the heart of the sea; the Lord of hosts is with us; the God of Jacob is our stronghold.

Psalm 61:1-2 Hear my cry, O God; give heed to my prayer. From the end of the earth I call to You when my heart is faint; lead me to the rock that is higher than I.

Isaiah 12:2 Behold, God is my salvation, I will trust and not be afraid. For the Lord God is my strength and my song, and He has become my salvation.

Jeremiah 17:7 Blessed is the man who trusts in the Lord and whose trust is the Lord.

Jeremiah 29:11-13 "For I know the plans I have for you," declares the Lord, "plans for welfare and not for calamity to give you a future and a hope. Then you will call upon Me and come and pray to Me, and I will listen to you. You will seek Me and find Me when you search for Me with all your heart."

Jeremiah 32:27 Behold, I am the Lord, the God of all flesh; is anything too difficult for Me?

Zechariah 4:6b "Not by might nor by power, but by My Spirit," says the Lord of hosts.

Matthew 6:27 And who of you by being worried can add a single hour to his life?

Matthew 6:33 But seek first His kingdom and His righteousness, and all these things will be added to you.

Matthew 6:34 So do not worry about tomorrow; for tomorrow will care for itself. Each day has enough trouble of its own.

Matthew 10:28 Do not fear those who kill the body but are unable to kill the soul; but rather fear Him who is able to destroy both soul and body in hell.

Matthew 19:26 And looking at *them* Jesus said to them, "With people this is impossible, but with God all things are possible."

Romans 8:28 And we know that God causes all things to work together for good to those who love God, to those who are called according to His purpose.

Romans 5:3-5 And not only this, but we also exult in our tribulations, knowing that tribulation brings about perseverance; and perseverance, proven character; and proven character, hope; and hope does not disappoint, because the love of God has been poured out within our hearts through the Holy Spirit who was given to us.

Romans 8:35–37 Who will separate us from the love of Christ? Will tribulation, or distress, or persecution, or famine, or nakedness, or peril, or sword? Just as it is written, for your sake we are being put to death all day long; we were considered as sheep to be slaughtered." But in all these things we overwhelmingly conquer through Him who loved us.

Philippians 1:21 For to me, to live is Christ and to die is gain.

1 John 4:4 You are from God, little children, and have overcome them; because greater is He who is in you than he who is in the world.

See also: greed/lust, anger, discontentment, judgment, and insecurity.

Appendix: Boundaries

In the past, it never occurred to me to restrict my eating when I wasn't on a diet. On the contrary, non-diet life was my opportunity to live it up—to eat *what* I wanted *when* I wanted without regard for the consequences.

It took me awhile to figure out that that was a bad way to live life. That life was actually *better* when I ate with control.

I don't know why it took so long. After all, I exercised control in other areas of my life: I was faithful to my husband. I paid off my credit card each month. I didn't say every single little thing that popped into my mind.

So why not also control my eating? Not just when I was on a diet, but all the time. In other words, lifelong boundaries in the area of food.

Lifelong Boundaries

According to freedictionary.com, a boundary is *something that indicates a border or a limit*. A playground fence is an example of a boundary. It limits where the kids can play. But that's not all it does. It also cramps their style.

Those little kids would love to run out in the street and look at all those fun, noisy cars—but the fence holds them in and says, "No, kids, you can't play in the street."

That doesn't mean the fence is bad. On the contrary, the fence makes their lives *better* because it protects them from harm.

The same is true for us. Lifelong boundaries in the area of food make our lives *better* because they keep us safe. Yes, they cramp our style, but you know what? Our style needs to be cramped. Because there are consequences to eating "what we want when we want." Here are a few of them:

Clothes that don't fit. Discomfort. Diabetes. Sore joints. Weight gain. Depression. Heart disease. Hopelessness. An early death . . . these are just a few of the enemies that lurk outside the "fence" of our boundaries waiting to destroy us.

There are several ways to limit eating long-term, but I'll just give a summary of the three most common types of boundaries.

Hunger Only

First, you can limit how often you eat by hunger—in other words, eat only when you're hungry and stop when you're full.

The advantage of this plan is that you can eat whenever you're hungry, and it's a natural way to control your weight.

The disadvantage is that you may not be hungry when you want to be hungry (like when all your friends are going out for ice cream or when your family is sitting down to dinner).

If you choose this option, you'll have to learn how to plan your meals and snacks so that you're hungry when you want to be.

Meals and Snacks

Another way to limit eating is to have a set number of meals and snacks each day. This is what I do. My boundaries are three meals and one snack a day.

The advantage of this is that it fits easily into life. You can eat with your family and also have a snack available for those unexpected eating occasions.

The disadvantage is that it's not a guarantee of weight loss and maintenance. You could gain weight on three meals and a snack if your meals and snacks are too big.

If you choose this option, you'll need to have a general idea of how much you can eat and still maintain your weight.

You'll also need to plan what you're going to eat *before* you sit down. If you eat something you didn't plan on eating (a second helping, for example), consider that a breaking of the boundaries and renew your mind.

Points or Calories

Another way to limit eating is to count points or calories. The advantage of this system is that you know exactly what you're eating.

The disadvantage is that you have to go to all the work of counting the points and calories, and if you're a perfectionist, you could become obsessed with points and calories. If this is your tendency, think about choosing one of the other options.

How to Choose Boundaries

If you're having a hard time deciding which boundaries to choose, ask yourself this question: *What can I live with for the rest of my life?*

Your boundaries should be loose enough that you can live with them on a permanent basis but strict enough that you won't be able to eat just for fun or for emotional reasons.

Think about your lifestyle, eating preferences, and health concerns when setting up your boundaries, and be sure to talk to your doctor first if you have medical issues.

Are Lifelong Boundaries The Answer?

If you're a perfectionist, you might be thinking, *I have to come up with the perfect boundaries if I want this to work.* This isn't true because we're transformed by the renewing of the mind, not by finding the perfect boundaries.

Make a commitment to renew your mind every time you break your boundaries. The questions and Bible verses in this book make that easy to do.

A Word of Caution

I can't close this section without a word to those of you who are tempted to eat too little. If you have ever struggled with anorexia or other eating disorders, or if you have friends and family telling you that you eat too little or that you're too skinny, please speak with a health professional. Don't use this book to try to get yourself to follow boundaries God doesn't want you to follow.

Just as we can believe lies that make us eat too much, we can also believe lies that make us eat too little. It's dangerous to eat too little. It can affect bone density, brain development, and a host of other areas I'm not capable of addressing as I am not a health care professional.

Don't believe the lie that you look fat when you really don't. Listen to your family. Listen to your friends. And learn to see yourself through God's eyes.

He loves you, and He wants what's best for you. And a too skinny body is not what's best! Rest in His love and work on getting rid of those lies that say you have to be skinny, skinny, skinny. God wants you to be at a healthy weight.

I DESERVE A DONUT

ABOUT THE AUTHOR

Barb Raveling is the author of *Freedom from Emotional Eating* and the *I Deserve a Donut* Christian weight loss app. She blogs about the renewing of the mind at barbraveling.com. Barb lives in Montana with her husband and the youngest of their four children. After homeschooling for 21 years, she and her husband are about to experience the empty nest. They hope they survive! In her spare time, she likes to camp, hike, eat (within her boundaries!), read, and hang out with family and friends.

Made in the USA
Middletown, DE
05 November 2016